*Abies koreana 'Nana'*

UK Price £4.95

# AN ILLUSTRATED GUIDE TO

# CONIFERS

**Discover the fascination of growing conifers with this magnificent selection for the garden**

*Pinus ponderosa – male flowers*

*Pinus contorta latifolia*

# AN ILLUSTRATED GUIDE TO
# CONIFERS

**Discover the fascination of growing conifers with this magnificent selection for the garden**

## David Papworth

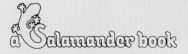

Published by Salamander Books Limited
LONDON

# A Salamander Book

© 1983 Salamander Books Ltd.,
27 Old Gloucester Street,
London WC1N 3AF,
United Kingdom.

ISBN 0 86101 193 7

Distributed in the UK by
Hodder & Stoughton Services,
P.O. Box 6, Mill Road, Dunton Green,
Sevenoaks, Kent TN13 2XX.

All correspondence concerning the
content of this volume should be
addressed to Salamander Books Ltd.

# Contents

Text and colour photographs are cross-referenced throughout as follows: 64 ◗. The plants are arranged in alphabetical order of Latin name. Page numbers in **bold** refer to text entries; those in *italics* refer to photographs.

# Credits

**Authors:** David Papworth is a freelance writer and illustrator on horicultural subjects. For a period of 12 years he was Gardening Editor of *Ideal Home* magazine. David has written several books, including *Patios and Water Gardening* and *Patios and Windowbox Gardening,* and the Salamander *Guide to Bulbs.* He regularly contributes articles and illustrations to gardening and DIY books and magazines.

**Editor:** Geoffrey Rogers
**Designer:** Letitia Tunstall
**Colour and monochrome reproductions:** David Bruce Graphics, England.
**Filmset:** SX Composing Ltd., England.

Printed in Belgium by
Henri Proost & Cie, Turnhout.

# Introduction

I wish there was a simple answer to the question: 'What are conifers?' but there is not. Some are cone-bearers, such as the pines; others have berries, such as the yews; and others have fruit-like seed cases. Some are evergreen, but not all. They all have resinous glands, but some other trees also produce resin. Some conifers have needle-like foliage, but others have flat leaves, and some are scale-like. The main characteristic in common is the strong central stem from which other branches radiate, but in some of the dwarf and prostrate varieties this is difficult to see. Without going into a more complex biological explanation and using very technical language it is difficult to explain what conifers are. Let us say that it includes the pines, firs, cupressus, cedars, larches and junipers, with the addition of a few other minor groups.

In the wild most conifers make upright trees with the shape of a column, cone, or pyramid. Due to local conditions, such as desert, mountain or arctic areas where there is little nutrition, harsh temperatures and constricted root area, a few species have become dwarfed. From these few hundred wild plants have been developed the thousands of cultivated trees and shrubs with a wide variety of forms and colours. The expert grower searches out a plant malformation, such as unusually pale colour, a cluster of tight growth, or a branch that tries to grow in the wrong direction. This is removed and used to propagate more plants of the same habit through cuttings. The demand for smaller plants to fit into the tiny gardens that are available with new housing developments today means that there is a ready market for slow-growing and dwarf conifers.

With the need for good-looking, low-maintenance gardens more gardeners are turning to conifers to provide a simple answer, interplanted with shrubs or heathers and used as ground cover. Conifers give an interesting planting with no lawn to mow or edges to trim and requiring very little care, no flowers to plant and lift as the season demands but a pleasant garden that looks good in all seasons.

Most conifers are easy to grow with little maintenance during the year: there are few leaves to sweep up and negligible pruning; pests and diseases are minimal; and provided the hardier varieties are grown there is little trouble from drought, wind or cold once the plants are established.

## Where to plant conifers

The garden designer usually relies on conifers to provide the backbone of the planting plan; they provide a basic structure that is there all the year, with tall, round or flat shapes of a constant colour and form around which to add other plants and develop seasonal changes of colour and pattern. In fact there are a few gardeners who will grow *only* evergreen trees and shrubs, because they find bare trunks and twigs, dead flowers and brown leaves depressing. But whatever image one has of the ideal garden, it should certainly contain at least a few conifers as a contrast to other plants.

Left: *A bed of conifers provides colour and interest throughout the year, usually with little or no maintenance. Their shapes and textures act as a superb background for showier seasonal plants.*

Small and dwarf conifers fit into a rockery and mix with other rockery plants, providing a vertical shape or horizontal accent that can make a necessary division between areas. Their distinctive form also acts as a fine contrast in a bed of heathers, the extra height making the bed more interesting and exciting to look at. The conifers usually remain a fairly constant colour, apart from some that sprout new growth in the spring; this can produce delightful fresh pale colours, and make candles, tassels or spots of interest on the plant.

The growth is usually slow, and the dwarf and slow-growing conifers will remain in scale with their surroundings for many years, although they may need replacing after twenty years or so, when they spread over other plantings. Some thrive in containers or sink gardens, where their roots are constricted and their size remains fairly constant.

Larger conifers come into their own as specimen plants in a border or set into the lawn, where they have plenty of space to spread and grow to their full height. It is wise to check on the ultimate height and age when choosing, as this can determine where to put them. Some take several centuries to mature and it could be that the house will disappear before the tree is fully grown.

## Buying conifers

When you buy conifers you will find that there are different ways in which they have been prepared. At first sight the difference is in the way the plant has been grown: it may be in a pot, or the roots may be wrapped up in hessian or polythene, and sometimes the roots are bare and just bundled up in some plastic. If you go to a reputable nursery there is usually a choice between the pot- or container-grown plant and one that has been grown in a nursery bed, lifted and the generous rootball wrapped to keep it moist. The container plant can be moved and planted at any time of year with little disturbance to the roots; this plant is more expensive than one with wrapped roots, which is normally for sale only in autumn or spring, when the plant is dormant and soil conditions are suitable. The cheapest plants are seedlings that are usually bundled together and sold primarily for hedging, and these have the minimum of soil around the roots; these give the highest rate of failure, but for anyone with a great deal of hedging to plant, this could be the only way to afford it.

When buying, choose a plant with a bright healthy appearance, and strong growth to the lower parts. The soil should fill the width of the pot or container and look as if it has been in this state for some time. Freshly moved soil suggests that the plant has been lifted out of a nursery bed and popped into a pot to command a higher price. Avoid plants that look tired, with the leaves drooping or browning, and with a rootball that is loose in the container. If it is sold as a rootball plant in hessian, make sure that the ball is moist and not dried up. Look for signs of insect attack and eggs left on the undersides of leaves; on stems and leaves watch for moulds, black spots and rusty markings and choose your conifers from those that are free of these.

Sometimes plants are offered with a marked difference in prices for similar plants, and this could be due to the nature of the propagation method. The cheapest way to grow plants is by seed; this is simply sown and the resulting seedlings are grown on to form saleable specimens. But some species either have no seed (being male plants) or the seed, if sown, will not grow true but will revert back to the original parent whose size and colour can vary widely; these species are usually grown from cuttings. Shoots are cut off the parent plant, one end is inserted into a cuttings mix that will encourage root growth, and the new plants are kept in a protected area for two or three years before being sold.

Certain cultivars are not very good when grown from cuttings, because their roots are poor and they can revert to a different colour or form; in this case, cuttings are taken and grafted onto a rootstock. This entails taking a cutting and slicing a clean angle on the stem; the rootstock is a small seedling with all its foliage removed and a similar angle cut on its stem. The two angles are put together and bound up to allow the sap to flow between the two parts. This union will gradually join up, often making a slight swelling on the stem. The plant is then grown on for up to four years to ensure that the union is satisfactory, before the plant is put on sale.

These grafted plants are the most labour-intensive, and understandably more expensive. When you examine your potential purchase do look at the stem for the tell-tale bulge that shows that it was propagated from a graft; this is a sign of a good plant, particularly with the named varieties of *Abies, Picea* and *Pinus*.

The middle-priced plants grown from cuttings are usually smooth-stemmed and are named varieties. The cheapest plants are those that grow well in the wild. Of course there are exceptions, such as

Below: **Picea abies 'Nidiformis'**
*This slow-growing dwarf cultivar is ideal for a rockery or small border.*
*It grows only 30cm (12in) high in 20 years, with a spread of 90cm (36in). Plant in sun or light shade.*

plants that are very rare, or whose seed has to be brought great distances, and in some instances the seed is very sparse and consequently expensive.

## Planting conifers

First it is important to choose the right place for your plant: an open site with the recommended amount of sun or shade, protection from winds and cold, the right type of soil with the correct level of moisture, and space to grow. Some places used for planting are most unsuitable. One house near where I am writing has a front garden that is 2m (6.5ft) from front door to gate, but squeezed into a narrow border along the path is a line of six *Cupressocyparis leylandii* to form a hedge. In three years they have grown over 1.8m (6ft) without any pruning or check on their growth, and if left to their own devices they will swamp the whole garden and cut off daylight from the front of the house completely.

The soil is important and can make the plant stunted or rampant. For most a soil that is in good heart, neither too acid nor too alkaline, moist but well drained is adequate. Some are particular about the amount of moisture, others are in need of protection from drought, and others require a deep soil rich in nutrients. Whichever soil you have, it is possible to improve the balance to suit most conifers. Generally the addition of peat, leaf-mould and bonemeal will help light sandy soils to retain more moisture, and if added to heavy clay soils they will increase the drainage and open the texture of the clay to enable plants to establish their roots.

If you have an acid soil that needs to be neutralized, the application of lime is beneficial. For alkaline soils the answer is plenty of wet peat, old pine needles, leaf-mould and a good dose of chelates of iron, usually sold as sequestrene. For the gardener who wants an easy life without the effort of soil conditioning it is simpler to choose a plant that will fit the soil, rather than making the soil fit the plant.

It is important to dig a hole bigger than the rootball. Weeds should be carefully removed, and the soil dug over to break it up to improve drainage; this is particularly important on clay soils. Fill the hole with water and let it drain away. Remove the container from the plant or take off the wrapping around the rootball, gently tease out the surface of the rootball to expose some of the fine hair-like roots, and place the ball in the hole. The soil level should be higher than the soil mark on the plant's stem, to encourage root growth and to help stabilize the whole plant. Fill in the hole, treading the soil down well to make sure that there are no air pockets around the roots. Then give another good dose of water, using a fine rose in order not to wash away the soil.

During the first year water the plant whenever the soil becomes dry: this includes wetting the foliage when there are drying winds. A layer of peat, pulverized bark or compost spread over the root area will help the plant to retain moisture during droughts. In a rockery this mulching could look wrong, and a generous layer of stone chips matching the surrounding area will make a good substitute.

Until the plant has established itself, it is wise to keep at least 30cm (12in) of soil around each conifer clear of weeds, to allow the plant to breathe. This is particularly important with slow-growing dwarf varieties, which can easily be overwhelmed and choked by other more vigorous plants growing close by.

## How healthy are conifers?

The health of conifers is normally quite good. There is a greater danger from drought, excess moisture and wrong soil conditions than from pests and diseases. They do occur, however, and normally they can be controlled with a spray of pesticide and fungicide. Forestry areas have problems when deer and rabbits cause damage, but unless you live in a very rural area where these animals roam freely, they can be ignored.

When using chemicals, make sure that you read the instructions properly and follow them exactly. Most garden chemicals have to pass a very stringent test for danger to the environment, but if the dilution, timing and method of application are not followed, the wrong insects can be killed, soil and plants spoilt, and your health endangered. There are newer and improved chemicals arriving on the market all the time and it is wise to check with your garden stockist to find out what old products have been superseded by better ones.

## Do conifers need pruning?

On the whole conifers need very little pruning. In fact, for some it is not recommended at all, as it can cause the cut branch to die back even further. Some conifers need just a little trimming to tidy their shape, but others are grown as hedges and require regular cutting to keep the hedge neat. The topiary enthusiast can train and clip conifers into the most extraordinary shapes, but use only those plants that will stand this treatment, such as yew.

Most conifers have their own particular form: some are column-like, others conical, some pyramidal; there are weeping forms, trailing or prostrate varieties, or even semi-prostrate ones where some branches try to grow upwards; and there are bun shapes and mound-forming plants. With these different types it is better to allow their forms to grow naturally.

## Why have I selected these conifers?

This is a personal selection to give a wide coverage of plants and their forms and foliage colours. With only space for 156 conifers from thousands, there are bound to be omissions, and to readers who find that their particular favourite is missing I extend my apologies. I have chosen plants that are commercially available: many will be for sale at the local garden centre, but for some you will need to write or go to a specialist grower who stocks the rarer specimens. Within these constraints, I hope I have managed a balance of sorts.

The use of Latin names is important because it is an international system. Common names vary from district to district and from country to country, and what is a white pine to one person is something completely different to another. It is easy to mix up firs and pines, and also to think that all plants with scale-like leaves are cupressus. The most usual common names are given after the Latin name and indexed separately at the back of the book.

Above: **Abies balsamea 'Hudsonia'**
*This slow-growing dwarf variety is ideal for planting in a rockery.* 17♦

Below: **Abies cephalonica 'Meyer's Dwarf'**
*A slow- and low-growing shrub suitable for the smaller garden.* 17♦

Above: **Abies concolor 'Glauca Compacta'**
*A highly recommended conifer for rockeries, containers or as a lawn specimen – wherever its attractive foliage can be seen to advantage.* 18♦

Above: **Abies lasiocarpa arizonica
'Compacta'**
This distinctive slow-growing conifer
has a fine colour and a dwarf habit,
making it ideal for planting in
rockeries and mixed borders. 18♦

Above: **Abies magnifica 'Glauca'**
*Grown for its unusual foliage colour,
this conifer will develop slowly into a
fine large specimen.* 19♦

Below: **Abies koreana 'Nana'**
*A dwarf Korean fir prized for its
prolific cones and attractive new
growth during the spring months.* 20♦

Above: **Cedrus deodara
'Golden Horizon'**
*The lovely golden foliage shines
beautifully during the spring.* 24▸

Below: **Abies procera
'Glauca Prostrata'**
*A magnificent cluster of large cones
borne amid fresh spring growth.* 21▸

# Abies balsamea 'Hudsonia'

*(Balsam fir)*
- **Provide shelter when young**
- **Deep moist soil**
- **Slow-growing small bush**

This variety forms a dwarf shrub up to 30cm (12in) tall in ten years, but can reach 75cm (30in) in 30 years. Branches and foliage form a dense, compact bush with a flattish top, spreading to almost 1m (39in) wide. In winter it has resinous buds; in spring these open and expose soft flat grey leaves that turn to mid-green as they mature during the summer.

This is an ideal rockery plant as it remains in scale with other rockery species. The cylindrical cones grow on the upper sides of the branches, and they open and break up when the seed is ripe.

Plant the seeds in late winter for extra stock. Avoid extremes of soil such as boggy situations, pure sand or chalk; but grow in a deep moist well-drained soil. Place in an area protected against hard frost, which can damage the young shoots. This variety is normally pest- and disease-free.

**Take care**
Avoid frost on young young shoots. 12♦

# Abies cephalonica

*(Grecian fir)*
- **Avoid frost pockets**
- **Moist soil with a little chalk**
- **Slow-growing large tree**

This species forms a large conical tree that can reach up to 30m (98ft). The shiny green leaves have white undersides that give a silvery appearance. The cylindrical cones stand up from the branches, and sometimes reach 18cm (7in) long.

The tree needs a deep moist soil, but not waterlogged. It will grow well in chalky soil, and can withstand fairly polluted air. Do not plant it where there are late frosts, as it breaks into growth early in the season and the young shoots are frost tender. These shoots, pale brown and hairless, sprout from the resinous winter buds. The plants make fine specimens but their size makes them unsuitable for the smaller garden. One cultivar, 'Meyer's Dwarf', is a slow- and low-growing spreading shrub.

Seeds can be collected from the open cones and sown in late winter in a seed compost; plant out after two or three years.

**Take care**
Allow plenty of room to grow. 12♦

# Abies concolor 'Glauca Compacta'

*(Colorado white fir)*
- **Stands heat and dry conditions**
- **Avoid chalky soils**
- **Slow-growing small bush**

This dwarf shrub from North America is one of the best conifers for the rock garden, or even as a specimen for a lawn or a container. It has silver-blue foliage that grows in a slightly irregular form, giving it an attractive character. It can take up to 25 years to reach 75cm (30in) tall, with a spread of just over 1m (39in). It prefers a deep moist soil but will tolerate hot and dry conditions; avoid a chalky soil. The winter buds are large and resinous, and open in spring to pale hairless clusters of leaves. The cones, almost 25cm (10in) long, are pale green when young but turn purple as they mature.

This shrub can be grown from seed, but the plants may vary in colour; it is normally propagated by grafting the right shade of leaf onto a dwarf rootstock. The plants are generally free from pests and diseases.

**Take care**
Avoid waterlogged sites. 13♦

# Abies grandis

*(Giant fir)*
- **Prefers humid conditions**
- **Deep moist soil**
- **Fast-growing large tree**

This fast-growing tree will grow to over 18m (59ft), and sometimes reaches 48m (157ft), forming a large cone with a spread of over 4.5m (15ft). The dark glossy green leaves are formed on each side of the stem, which gives it the appearance of a double-sided comb. The bright green cones are 10cm (4in) long. The tree forms fresh pale green shoots on the tips of the established dark green foliage in spring. The foliage has a pleasant perfume when crushed.

This tree will grow in a deep moist soil, and it can stand some lime. It is a good plant for a container while young, but should be planted out in a permanent position before it grows too large, for it needs plenty of space to form a good specimen tree.

It can be grown from seeds collected from the ripe cones; sow in early spring in a seed compost, and plant out after two or three years. Normally trouble-free.

**Take care**
Avoid dry and exposed sites.

# Abies koreana
*(Korean fir)*
- **Thrives in humid conditions**
- **Deep moist soil**
- **Slow-growing small tree**

This small neat slow-growing tree is very popular for its dark green leaves; for its prolific violet-purple cones, just over 5cm (2in) long; and for its slow growth. Used on rockeries or in a container, it will take over ten years to reach 3m (10ft), but where there is unrestricted space it may eventually reach 10m (33ft). The tree has a regular tapering shape. In spring, the new silvery grey leaves contrast with the darker blue-green mature growth. The cones are borne on the upper side of the branches and appear on quite young specimens. There are two dwarf-growing varieties, 'Compact Dwarf' and 'Nana', both suitable for rockeries.

When the seeds ripen they can be sown in a seed compost in early spring and left for two or three years before planting in their final positions. Grow in a deep moist soil that is free from chalk. This tree is both pest- and disease-free.

**Take care**
Avoid boggy soil conditions. 15♦

# Abies lasiocarpa arizonica
*(Cork fir)*
- **Prefers humid conditions**
- **Deep moist soil**
- **Slow-growing medium tree**

This medium-sized tree has thick corky bark, and its distinctive winter buds are white and resinous. It will reach 18m (59ft) tall where conditions are good, but the average plant reaches half this size. The leaves are silvery grey in colour; the smallish cones, 7.5cm (3in) long, are purple when young.

When the cones start to break up, collect the seed and sow in a seed compost in early spring. Allow the seedlings to grow on in a seed bed for over two years before planting out in their permanent positions. Plant this tree in a deep moist soil that is free or almost free from lime. A slow-growing dwarf cultivar, 'Compacta', has blue-grey foliage, and may take ten years to reach 70cm (28in)

Watch for white waxy wool on the leaves and branches, caused by adelgids; spray with malathion in late spring to control an attack. If the stems start to die back, spray the tree with a fungicide to deter fungus.

**Take care**
Avoid a waterlogged site. 14♦

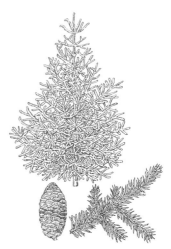

# Abies magnifica
*(Californian red fir)*
- Cool, moist summers and cold winters
- Avoid chalk or limy soil
- Slow-growing large tree

This slender tree thrives at high altitudes, and will reach a height of 60m (197ft) provided it has the right growing conditions and a soil free from chalk. It dislikes mild winters and lowland areas. The foliage is grey to blue-green, and there is a cultivar 'Glauca' that has deep green leaves covered wtih a grape-like bloom. The cones, up to 23cm (9in) long, are purple when young and turn to golden brown by autumn.

This tree can be grown from seed, which should be sown in winter in seed trays or outdoors in a seed bed in very early spring. When the seedlings are large enough to handle they should be transplanted into a nursery bed and grown on for at least two years before planting in their final positions.

Watch for tufts of white waxy wool on leaves and stems; these are caused by adelgids – insects related to the aphids; spray with malathion.

**Take care**
Give the young tree a good mulch each year until established. 15♦

# Abies pinsapo 'Glauca'
*(Spanish fir)*
- Suits most situations
- Will tolerate chalky soil
- Slow-growing large tree

Found in the mountains of Spain this medium to large tree is noted for its very short, stiff powder-blue needles, which are about 6mm (0.2in) long and arranged all round the branches. This tree will reach over 18m (59ft) tall but it will take a long time; after ten years it will have reached 3.7m (12ft), with a spread at the base of half this. The cones are about 15cm (6in) long, with a purplish hue when young but turning brown as they mature.

The Spanish fir can be grown as a container plant but will need to be planted out after a few years. It will stand most soils and situations except excessive moisture around the root system. It can be raised from seed, but for a good blue colour it is best to graft a piece of the desired parent onto *A. pinsapo* stock; keep it in a nursery bed for two or three years before planting out. Spray with malathion and a fungicide to keep troubles to a minimum.

**Take care**
Avoid waterlogged soil.

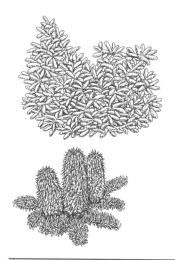

# Abies procera 'Glauca Prostrata'

*(Noble fir)*
- **Suits most situations**
- **Avoid chalky soil**
- **Slow-growing low bush**

This low-growing bush has parents that can reach 60m (197ft) and originates in the Western United States. The dwarf cultivar makes a fine specimen for the rockery or border. The blue-green leaves have a fine curled form, and the compact branches give it an interesting shape. The cones are brown, up to 25cm (10in) long, with downward-pointing green bracts that almost cover the cone.

It is best grown from grafted cuttings in order to keep a dwarf variety. These should be kept in a nursery bed for a few years before planting out in their final situation. Grow in a deep, moist but well-drained acid soil. If the leading shoot starts to grow vigorously it should be pruned in spring to keep a low shape.

Spray with malathion to keep the sap-sucking adelgids from attacking the plant, and use a fungicide to prevent fungal attack.

**Take care**
Watch for a vigorous leader and prune back. 16♦

# Agathis australis

*(Kauri pine)*
- **Needs a protected and mild situation**
- **Can stand a chalky soil**
- **Slow-growing large tree**

Its New Zealand rain-forest home provides this tree with ideal conditions that allow it to grow up to 50m (164ft), with the diameter of the trunk reaching 8m (26ft); but in areas of lower rainfall and colder temperatures the trees are dwarfed, and reach only about 5m (16.4ft) in ten years. The leathery leaves are flat, 5cm (2in) long by 1cm (0.4in) wide, and lime-green in colour. The bark is thick, scaly and resinous; if the surface is broken it bleeds a thick milky liquid. The ball-like cones are 7.5cm (3in) across.

The tree can be grown from seed sown in the spring; or cuttings taken from vertical shoots can be struck in a cold frame in an equal peat and sand mix, and grown on for three years before being planted out.

They are normally free from pests and diseases, but watch for honey fungus; small toadstools growing around the root area are an indication of trouble.

**Take care**
Avoid a cold frost pocket.

 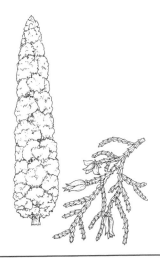

# Araucaria araucana

*(Monkey puzzle tree)*
- **Protect when young**
- **Moist loamy soil**
- **Medium-fast-growing tree that slows down**

This tree from South America used to be very popular, but is becoming more rare. Its well-known shape, and the branches covered with short, prickly, overlapping leaves, are very distinctive. Given good growing conditions it may reach 30m (98ft). The cones, about 15cm (6in) long, take up to three years to mature, falling to pieces when the 2.5cm (1in) seeds are ripe. Up to 200 seeds are contained in each cone, and these are edible.

The seeds can be sown in a moist soil in autumn; in light or heavy soils sow them in spring. Some protection should be given, as the young plants are frost-tender. After three years plant them out in their final situations. Initially they grow quite quickly, but slow down as the tree produces more branches and foliage.

These trees are normally free from pests and disease, but watch for toadstools around the tree base, which could indicate honey fungus.

**Take care**
Portect against frost when young.

# Calocedrus decurrens

*(Incense cedar)*
- **Most situations but prefers sun**
- **Moist well-drained soil**
- **Large tree with a medium growth rate**

This tree from the Western USA has a column-like appearance and will reach up to 45m (148ft) in good growing conditions. The dark green foliage is scaly, and extends down the stems forming fan-like sprays. The smooth, oval, woody cones are 2.5cm (1in) long; they hang under the branches and ripen the first year, releasing seed in autumn. The bark is pale brown, scaly and heavily ridged.

Seeds should be sown when they drop from the cone. Place them in a good seed compost, and plant out seedlings in the following spring; keep them for two or three years in a nursery bed before planting out in their final positions. Grow in moist but well-drained soil in a warm place; if the site is too exposed or the soil is poor, the tree will eventually lose some of its foliage and look untidy. Should the main stem fork, prune back to one leader to keep the form symmetrical.

**Take care**
Keep young plants moist.

# Cedrus atlantica

*(Atlas cedar)*
- **Most situations and seaside**
- **Good well-drained soil**
- **Large tree, quick-growing when young**

These originate in the Atlas Mountains of Algeria and Morocco. The handsome trees sometimes reach 36m (118ft) tall, but more often grow to half this height, with a spread of 4.5m (15ft). They thrive in a poor soil; but if the soil is rich and the area warm, these conditions promote a lank growth that gives the tree a weeping habit. The bunches of needles are dark green. The cones are about 7.5cm (3in) long by 5cm (2in) wide, changing from green to dark brown as they ripen.

Seeds can be sown in early spring, and transplanted into nursery beds when the seedlings are about 7.5cm (3in) tall. Grow on for a few years, then plant out in their final positions. Grow in a good well-drained soil that has leaf-mould, peat and bonemeal added. Keep a single leader until the required height is reached, then prune to keep this size; when the lowest branches die, cut back flush to the trunk.

**Take care**
Do not grow this in a small garden.

# Cedrus atlantica 'Glauca Pendula'

*(Weeping blue cedar)*
- **Grows in most situations**
- **Well-drained garden soil**
- **Slow-growing small tree**

This tree originated at Chatenay, near Paris, a hundred years ago, when a weeping form was grafted onto a standard that had come from parents from the Atlas Mountains of Algeria and Morocco. The tree is slow-growing and forms a beautiful weeping shape of blue-needled foliage that should, after a century or so, make a wide spreading tree some 12m (39ft) across and 4.5m (15ft) tall. The cones are up to 7.5cm (3in) long and 5cm (2in) wide, changing from blue-green to brown.

The best plants are available from reputable nurseries, as it is a highly specialized procedure to achieve a good-shaped plant. A weeping form has to be grafted onto a standard of at least 2m (6.5ft) tall, to give it some height and allow the weeping branches to be trained horizontally and then trail down to the ground. Grow in a well-drained soil that has had plenty of peat, leaf-mould and bonemeal added.

**Take care**
Support the branches.

# Cedrus deodara 'Aurea'

*(Golden Himalayan cedar)*
- **Light shade when young**
- **Good well-drained soil**
- **Slow-growing medium tree**

This beautiful yellow-foliaged tree from the Himalayas has a drooping character. It has longer needles than other cedars, about 5cm (2in). The golden colour is noticeable on exposed foliage but becomes more green where strong light does not penetrate. The yellow is less pronounced in winter. The tree grows to 3m (10ft) tall in ten years, but can eventually reach 12m (39ft). The cultivar 'Golden Horizon' is a semi-prostrate variety, reaching 75cm (30in) tall and twice as wide.

Seeds can be sown in seed compost in spring; when the seedlings are 7.5cm (3in) tall, plant them out in a nursery bed. Keep them in a lightly shaded area, as this variety is prone to frost damage when young. Plant out in the final positions after three or four years; stake plants over 45cm (18in) tall. The soil should be well-drained, with leaf-mould, peat and bonemeal.

**Take care**
Do not plant young trees in frost pockets; they are tender. 16♦

# Cedrus deodara 'Pendula'

- **Light shade when young**
- **Well-drained garden soil**
- **Slow-growing low shrub**

The parents of this shrub come from the Himalayas, and are noted for their 5cm (2in) needles and low habit. Left to itself, it spreads over the soil to cover an area of some 2m (6.5ft) across; but it can be trained upwards on a structure or grafted onto an upright stock to form a truly pendulous tree. The deep green foliage has a blue bloom when young. The cones, up to 10cm (4in) long, take two years to mature.

To propagate, graft a cutting of the parent plant onto a young cedar seedling of dwarf habit; in this way the growth character of the parent is kept. When plants have grown on for several months, plant them out in nursery beds, where they should stay for three years before being planted out in their final positions. The soil should be well-drained and enriched with humus.

Normally, these plants are free from pest and disease attack.

**Take care**
Avoid frost-prone areas for young plants; they may be damaged.

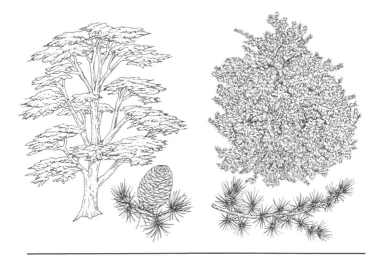

## Cedrus libani
*(Cedar of Lebanon)*
- **Prefers a warm dry position**
- **Ordinary well-drained soil**
- **Slow-growing large tree**

This species from Asia Minor and Syria is well-known for its Biblical connections. It forms a conical tree in the first few decades, but matures into the well-known flat-topped form with horizontal branches. It will eventually reach well over 36m (118ft), but in 20 years it can make 12m (39ft) with a spread of 7.5m (25ft), growing quite quickly to start with but slowing down as it matures. The foliage is dark green and has short needles. The purplish green cones are up to 15cm (6in) long and take two years to ripen on the tree.

The seed should be sown in a good seed compost. Plant out into a nursery bed when the seedlings reach 7.5cm (3in) tall; they should be left for three or four years before being planted out into final situations. They prefer a warm, dry site. Care must be taken to support the large lower branches of mature trees after snow, as the weight can break them.

**Take care**
Clear snow from the lower branches of mature trees. 33♦

## Cedrus libani 'Nana'
*(Dwarf Lebanon cedar)*
- **Prefers a warm dry place**
- **Well-drained garden soil**
- **Slow-growing small bush**

The original dwarf varieties were probably found growing in restricted pockets of soil. These have been cultivated and now there are various dwarf forms known as 'Nana', all fairly similar with a bushy shape, slow-growing and dense. They will reach a height of about 1m (39in) with a similar spread, but with a growth rate of around 2.5cm (1in) a year they take some time to reach full size. The small needles are dark or greyish green. A little pruning is needed to keep the form; remove some branches to prevent overcrowding. This is an ideal bush for rockeries, sink gardens, containers or borders.

Graft these plants a minimum of three years before planting out into their final positions, to make sure that the graft is firmly established. Plant in a soil enriched with peat, leaf-mould and bonemeal, and keep weed-free for the first few years.

**Take care**
Keep in shape with careful pruning during the autumn. 34-5♦

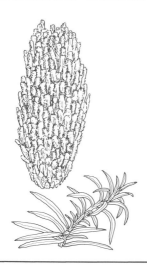

# Cephalotaxus harringtonia 'Fastigiata'

*(Upright Japanese plumyew)*
- Grows in shade
- Prefers chalky soil
- Slow-growing small tree

Originating probably in China but cultivated for several centuries in Japan, this small tree has an upright form with the appearance of a large-leaved variety of *Taxus baccata 'Fastigiata'*, the Irish Yew. Its very dark green leaves, up to 6.4cm (2.5in) long, are arranged around the vertical stems. The tree is slow-growing to start with; it will grow to 1.5m (5ft) in ten years and eventually 5m (16.4ft). There are male and female trees, and the 2.5cm (1in) cones appear on females.

Seeds can be sown in a seed compost in autumn; plant out the seedlings in a nursery bed when they are about 7.5cm (3in) tall, and grow on for two or three years before planting them out in their final situations. This tree will grow in shade even under other trees.

This variety may be attacked by scale insects, which should be sprayed with malathion as a control.

## Take care
Avoid waterlogged soil. 34♦

# Chamaecyparis lawsoniana 'Aurea Densa'

- Open situation
- Ordinary garden soil
- Very slow-growing dwarf bush

The parents of this plant originated in the Western USA, but this particular form was raised in England in 1939. The dwarf golden-leaved plant grows to 2m (6.5ft), but will take about 30 years to reach half this height. It is ideal for the rockery, container, sink garden or border, where its densely packed fans of flattened leaves and its regular conical shape will be seen to advantage. It has tiny green cones about 6mm (0.2in) in diameter, which turn brown as they ripen.

The seeds can be sown, but seedlings can vary a lot. It is better to take cuttings, in an equal mix of peat and sand in a cold frame in spring. Transplant them into nursery beds in autumn and grow on for three years before moving to their final situation.

Normally these plants are free from pests and diseases except for honey fungus.

## Take care
Keep an area around the young plant free from weeds and other plants. 35♦

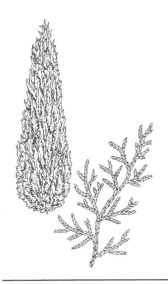

# Chamaecyparis lawsoniana 'Columnaris'

- Light shade or open site
- Well-drained garden soil
- Slow-growing small tree

This variety was raised in Holland in about 1940, from Western United States parentage, and is regarded as one of the best blue narrow small trees, ideal for the smaller garden. The upward-facing fans of scale-like leaves give it an upright form. It is slow-growing, reaching 2.4m (8ft) tall and 80cm (32in) wide in ten years if the weather and soil conditions are right, but growing slower and making a narrower plant where conditions are harder. It should reach a height of 4.5m (15ft) in 20 years.

To keep as pure a colour as possible, it should be propagated by taking cuttings in midwinter or late spring; put these into an equal mix of peat and sand. Place the spring cuttings in a cold frame and the winter ones in a propagating frame, and leave until autumn. Those that have taken can be planted out in a nursery bed for three years before being put into their final positions.

**Take care**
Keep the nursery bed weed-free.

# Chamaecyparis lawsoniana 'Elegantissima'

- Open situation
- Well-drained garden soil
- Small tree with medium growth

This cultivar was raised in England around 1920, and forms a graceful small tree of a pyramid shape. It makes a fine specimen for the medium or small garden, reaching only 2.4m (8ft) in ten years. The foliage varies from cream to silvery grey, but for a bright colour keep it in the open so that plenty of light reaches the plant. The green cones are only 6mm (0.2in) across, and they turn brown as the seeds ripen.

The seeds can be sown but there is likely to be a wide variation in the seedlings, of both form and colour; keep the best examples and discard the rest. When the seedlings have been kept in a nursery bed for three years, the best can be planted out in their final positions. Alternatively, cuttings can be taken and set in an equal mix of sand and peat; set the rooted cuttings in a nursery bed for three years, and then plant out.

**Take care**
Keep in sunlight for good colour.

27

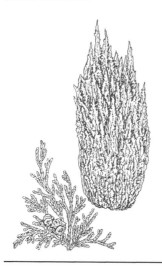 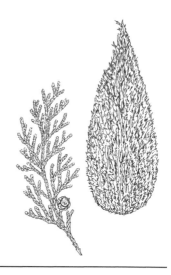

# Chamaecyparis lawsoniana 'Elwoodii'

- Open or lightly shaded site
- Well-drained garden soil
- Slow-growing bush

Probably one of the best-known cultivars of its family, this is ideal for the small garden and rockery. It is of garden origin from cross-pollination of other cultivars developed from the Western United States parents. It has a fine blue-green colour, and a column-like shape with tight neat foliage on an upright branch system. In ten years it can reach 2m (6.5ft) tall and 75cm (30in) wide; in 20 years it reaches 3m (10ft). It can be made to grow more slowly by lifting it each year and replanting in autumn. The cones are green, changing to brown as they ripen.

The seeds can be sown, but are unlikely to be true to type. Some growers sow plenty of seed and retain only seedlings that show the colour and characteristics of the parent. To obtain a plant true to its parent, cuttings should be taken; after they root, keep them in a nursery bed for three years.

**Take care**
Prune to keep a single leader for a well-shaped bush. 35♦

# Chamaecyparis lawsoniana 'Erecta'

- Light shade or open position
- Ordinary garden soil
- Medium to large tree with medium growth rate

This conifer was raised over 100 years ago from strains of its Western United States parents. It has very distinctive bright green foliage, and an upright conical habit with upward-facing fans of scale-like leaves. It grows to 2m (6.5ft) tall and 75cm (30in) wide in ten years, to 9m (29.5ft) in 20 years, and to well over 15m (49ft) in 100 years. It is useful as a hedge plant provided it is kept trimmed to size. The cones are only 6mm (0.2in) across, and are green in colour, ripening to brown.

The seeds can be sown, and the brightest green seedlings selected to grow on in a nursery bed for three years, when they will be 7.5cm (3in) tall. The best specimens can then be planted out in their final positions. This tree will grow well in ordinary soil in light shade as well as in sunshine. To encourage a good root system and early growth, add peat, leaf-mould and bonemeal to the soil.

**Take care**
Avoid snow making the branches spread, by shaking off heavy falls.

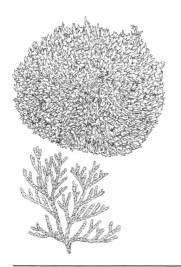

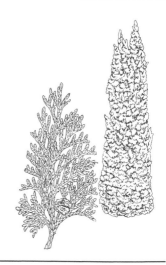

# Chamaecyparis lawsoniana 'Green Globe'

- Open or lightly shaded site
- Ordinary well-drained soil
- Slow-growing dwarf bush

This dwarf variety was raised in New Zealand from United States parents. It is the most compact of the dwarf varieties available. Its fine green colour, combined with its globular form, makes it ideal for a rockery, sink garden, container or border where it can be viewed clearly. It will reach 30cm (12in) in ten years, and should eventually reach twice this size. The sprays of green leaves give a softer outline than that of some other miniature forms. The green cones are 6mm (0.2in) wide, and turn brown as they ripen.

The seed can be sown, but is unlikely to come true. It is better to take cuttings or to graft onto a dwarf stock. Cuttings should be placed in an equal mixture of peat and sand, and when rooted, transplanted into a nursery bed to grow on for three years. Keep the bed well weeded, and then plant them out in their final situations. Place either in the open or in light shade.

**Take care**
Keep young plants well weeded. 37♦

# Chamaecyparis lawsoniana 'Lutea'

- Sheltered open situation
- Well-drained garden soil
- Medium-sized tree with medium rate of growth

First appearing over 100 years ago, this tree originated from United States parents. It has a column-like shape with compact drooping branches and foliage, but for the first ten years it will look an irregular mass of foliage, reaching 2.4m (8ft) tall and wide. During the next ten years it will grow vertically with little increase in girth, to reach over 20m (66ft) tall. The leaf colour is a beautiful gold if it stands in the open and receives plenty of sunlight; but placed in a shady situation it becomes green. The 6mm (0.2in) cones are borne profusely on the upper branches.

The seeds can be sown in a good seed compost, but only very golden seedlings should be retained. Plant out into a nursery bed when they are 7.5cm (3in) tall. Grow on for three years before planting in their final positions.

Usually this tree is free from pests and diseases.

**Take care**
Avoid coastal areas; salt and wind make poor specimens. 36♦

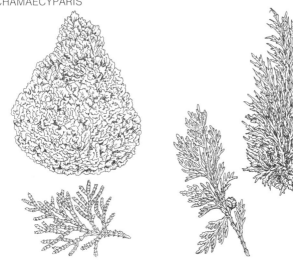

# Chamaecyparis lawsoniana 'Minima Aurea'

- Open situation
- Ordinary garden soil
- Slow-growing dwarf bush

This dwarf rounded bush was raised some 60 years ago. The main difference between this and 'Aurea Densa' is that the forms of foliage are mainly ranged vertically giving it a distinctive texture. Its rounded form is slightly taller than wide, reaching 50cm (20in) tall by 40cm (16in) wide in ten years, and just over 1m (39in) tall by 80cm (32in) wide in 30 years. The scale-like leaves are golden-yellow and soft to the touch; they need to be placed in open sunlight to retain their brightness. A rockery situation is ideal for both its colour and its size. The small cones are green, turning to brown when they ripen.

It is best to propagate by taking cuttings, which should be struck in spring and set in an equal mixture of peat and sand in a cold frame. Plant out the rooted cuttings into a nursery bed in autumn, grow on for three years, and then plant out.

**Take care**
Keep the nursery bed weed-free. 37♦

# Chamaecyparis lawsoniana 'Pembury Blue'

- Open or light shady position
- Well-drained garden soil
- Medium-sized tree

This cultivar, of recent introduction, is probably the bluest of all lawsonianas. Initially it forms an upright bush that develops into a column-like tree 3m (10ft) tall by 1m (39in) wide, with rather loose-looking fans of foliage; the eventual size is likely to be around 10m (33ft). The vivid silvery blue leaves are arranged in spiky vertical sprays, the upper branches bearing 6mm (0.2in) blue-green cones, which turn brown as they ripen.

It is best to propagate from cuttings. Press them into a mixture of half peat and half sand in spring, and keep them in a cold frame until autumn. They can then be transplanted into a nursery bed for three years, before being planted out in their final situations. Keep the nursery bed free from weeds, or the young plants may be starved of light and nourishment. Place in good well-drained soil with plenty of peat, leaf-mould and bonemeal added.

**Take care**
Clear tree of heavy snow. 38♦

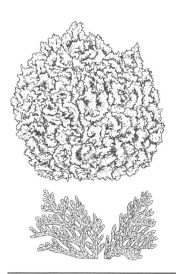

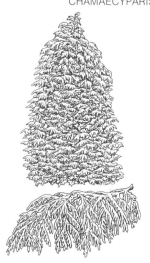

# Chamaecyparis lawsoniana 'Pygmaea Argentea'
- Shelter from wind and frost
- Ordinary garden soil
- Very slow-growing dwarf bush

A dwarf variegated bush of rounded shape, also known as 'Backhouse Silver'. Very slow-growing, it will reach only 38cm (15in) tall and wide in ten years, and about 1m (39in) when fully mature. The foliage is dark green with a dusting of creamy white around the perimeter of each spray, which looks rather startling, particularly if the plant is placed in a sunny position to keep the blonde edges pale. In winter there is the possibility of some burn on the leaves from frost and wind, but they normally recover in spring. It makes an ideal plant for a rockery, sink garden, or container where it can be seen to advantage.

Propagate from cuttings or by grafting. The cuttings should be struck in spring, transplanted in autumn, and grown on for three years before being planted out.

Generally this bush is free from pests and diseases.

**Take care**
Young plants may be choked by weeds or larger plants. 39♦

# Chamaecyparis lawsoniana 'Stewartii'
- Open site
- Well-drained garden soil
- Medium to large tree of medium growth rate

This attractive golden cultivar of *Chamaecyparis lawsoniana* originated in the Western United States. It will form a medium to large conical tree, which in 20 years should grow to 9m (29.5ft) tall with a spread of 2.4m (8ft). The branches have flattened fans of golden-yellow leaves that fade to yellow-green during the winter months. It is hardy, without foliage burn in winter from frost and wind. The green cones are 6mm (0.2in) wide, and turn brown as they ripen.

Seed can be sown, but wide variations from the parent can be expected, and it is better to grow plants from cuttings. These should be taken in spring, put into a half peat, half sand mixture, and kept in a cold frame until autumn; the rooted cuttings can then be planted out into a nursery bed and grown on for three years before planting out in their final positions. Normally they are free from pests and diseases.

**Take care**
Grow in open sunlight. 38-9♦

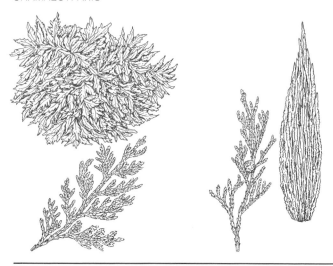

## Chamaecyparis lawsoniana 'Tamariscifolia'

- Open site or light shade
- Well-drained garden soil
- Slow-growing compact bush

This plant was raised in England in the 1920s and forms a medium-sized compact bush. It is unkempt when young, as the branches have no distinct form and grow anywhere; but when mature it becomes rounded with a flat top. The branches spread with flat sprays of blue-green leaves, to form a bush about 1.2m (4ft) tall and 70cm (28in) wide after ten years, and it can eventually reach over 5m (16.4ft) in 60 years. The cones, 6mm (0.2in) across, are green, gradually turning to brown.

The seeds can be sown, but it is unlikely that seedlings will be true to the parent. It is better to take cuttings, and set them in an equal sand and peat mix. When they have rooted, plant them out into a nursery bed and grow on for three years before transplanting into their final positions. Place in well-drained garden soil enriched with peat, leaf-mould and bonemeal.

**Take care**
Do not let young plants become choked with weeds. 40♦

## Chamaecyparis lawsoniana 'Witzeliana'

- Sunshine or light shade
- Ordinary garden soil
- Slow-growing small tree

This cultivar is similar to 'Erecta', but smaller, slower growing and with darker foliage. It has a narrow column-like form, with vertical branches and sprays of vivid green leaves. Likely to reach over 2m (6.5ft) tall with a spread of 50cm (20in) in ten years, it is ideal for the smaller garden or rockery where a strong but smallish vertical plant is required. The cones are 6mm (0.2in) wide, and mature from green to brown as the seed ripens.

It is unlikely that the seeds will grow true to the parent, and it is advisable to propagate from cuttings. Set these in half peat and half sand until rooted, then plant out into a nursery bed. After three years they can be placed in their final situations. The site should be open or have light shade, and the free-draining soil should have peat, leaf-mould and bonemeal added to give the plants a good start.

**Take care**
Keep the seedlings moist.

Above: **Cedrus libani**
*The well-known Cedar of Lebanon, a large tree that will take many years to mature and should be planted with plenty of space around it. Suitable only for the larger garden or park.* 25▸

Left: **Cephalotaxus harringtonia 'Fastigiata'**
*This slow-growing small tree forms a neat upright shape.* 26♦

Right: **Chamaecyparis lawsoniana 'Aurea Densa'**
*A dense, slow-growing dwarf cultivar for rockeries and containers.* 26♦

Far right: **Chamaecyparis lawsoniana 'Elwoodii'**
*A slow-growing bush with a neat shape. Popular for small gardens.* 28♦

Below: **Cedrus libani 'Nana'**
*This dwarf variety of the Cedar of Lebanon develops slowly into a dense bush. Prune it carefully during the autumn to keep it looking tidy.* 25♦

Above: **Chamaecyparis lawsoniana 'Lutea'**
*A golden tree of medium height and* growth, this variety needs a sunny location to keep its full colour. Protect it from strong winds. 29▶

Above: **Chamaecyparis lawsoniana 'Minima Aurea'**
*An attractive dwarf cultivar with distinctive 'vertical' foliage.* 30♦

Below: **'Chamaecyparis lawsoniana 'Green Globe'**
*A superb compact conifer of fine green colour and soft texture.* 29♦

Left: **Chamaecyparis lawsoniana 'Pembury Blue'**
*This beautiful cultivar will grow into a medium-sized tree and makes a fine specimen plant for the average garden. The distinctive foliage is probably the bluest in conifers.* 30♦

Right: **Chamaecyparis lawsoniana 'Pygmaea Argentea'**
*A variegated dwarf bush that excels as a focal point in the garden. Grow it in open sunshine to maintain the pale-edged foliage, but protect it from frost and cold winds.* 31♦

Below: **Chamaecyparis lawsoniana 'Stewartii'**
*This golden cultivar develops at a medium pace into a large tree. An open site in full sun will help to maintain the bright foliage colour.* 31♦

Left: **Chamaecyparis lawsoniana 'Tamariscifolia'**
*A slow-growing compact bush that eventually develops a rounded form. It looks best set among large rocks, where its colour and shape form a striking focal point.* 32♦

Right: **Chamaecyparis nootkatensis 'Pendula'**
*This graceful conifer develops at a steady pace into an attractive medium-sized tree. It will grow in sun or light shade and thrives well in moist soils close to water.* 49♦

Below: **Chamaecyparis obtusa 'Nana'**
*An extremely slow-growing dwarf bush with distinctive saucer-shaped fans of dense green foliage. A superb subject for rockeries and miniature gardens.* 50♦

Above: **Chamaecyparis pisifera 'Filifera Aurea'**
*Prized for its thread-like golden foliage, this slow-growing cultivar will develop into a large shrub.* 51♦

Far left: **Chamaecyparis obtusa 'Nana Gracilis'**
*Widely used for Bonsai culture, this lovely Japanese cultivar will grace a rockery with its dark foliage.* 50♦

Left: **Chamaecyparis pisifera 'Boulevard'**
*Quick-growing but easily trimmed to size, this conifer is justifiably popular for its steely blue foliage.* 51♦

Right: **Chamaecyparis pisifera 'Plumosa Aurea'**
*This quick-growing small tree shines with colour in a sunny position.* 52♦

Left: **Chamaecyparis pisifera 'Snow'**
*Named for its pale green foliage with snow-like white tips, this slow-growing dwarf bush will thrive in a sheltered position out of sun.* 52♦

Right: **Cryptomeria japonica 'Bandai-sugi'**
*The combination of tight moss-like foliage and normal leaf growth gives this dwarf, slow-growing Japanese cultivar a unique appearance.* 54♦

Below: **Cryptomeria japonica 'Elegans'**
*This upright small tree changes in colour from blue-green during the summer to bronze or purple in the winter months. It grows quickly at first, then slows down.* 54♦

Above: **Cryptomeria japonica 'Vilmoriniana'**
*The tight foliage of this dwarf bush turns reddish purple in winter.* 55♦

Below: **Cryptomeria japonica 'Spiralis'**
*Twisted ringlets of dense foliage adorn this slow-growing bush.* 55♦

Above: **Cunninghamia lanceolata**
This conifer forms a tall graceful tree
with long pointed leaves. It is ideal as
a specimen planted in a lawn, where
it can grow steadily to a height of
about 4m (13ft) in ten years. 56♦

Above: **Cupressocyparis leylandii**
This is probably the best-known of
the conifers used for hedging.

*Raised about a hundred years ago, it
is very fast-growing, hardy, and
thrives in most types of soil.* 56♦

# Chamaecyparis nootkatensis 'Pendula'

- ● Open site or light shade
- ● Ordinary or boggy soil
- ● Medium-sized tree

This tree comes from the 'Nootka' or 'Alaskan' cypress, but differs from its parent by being smaller and having long graceful foliage that gives it a weeping habit. It forms a medium-sized tree about 10m (33ft) tall, but if conditions are ideal, with moisture and nutrients available, it can grow to over 18m (59ft). In ten years it should reach 3m (10ft) tall, with a spread of 1m (39in). It makes a fine focal point in a large garden. The cones, about 1.2cm (0.5in) wide, are noted for their spiked scales, and turn from green to brown in their second year as the seeds ripen.

The seeds can be sown, but are unlikely to be true to the parent. It is wiser to use cuttings, setting them in a half and half mixture of peat and sand; when rooted, transfer them to a nursery bed for three years, and then plant them out into their final positions. Use a moist or well-drained soil with peat, leaf-mould and bonemeal added.

**Take care**
Plant in an open area for effect. 4141▶

# Chamaecyparis obtusa 'Crippsii'

*(Golden Hinoki cypress)*
- ● Open situation
- ● Ordinary well-drained soil
- ● Slow-growing small tree

Originating from Japanese parents, this plant has a beautiful shape and colour. It will reach a height of 3m (10ft) with a spread of 1.2m (4ft) in ten years, and has a mature height of 10m (33ft). It is loosely conical in shape, with sprays of golden-yellow leaves that give off a resinous scent when crushed. The cones are about 1cm (0.4in) across, with eight scales with small points, and they ripen in the first year.

The seeds can be sown, but colour and form can vary. It is better to grow from cuttings, which should be set in a half peat, half sand mixture until rooted. Then plant them out into a nursery bed for three years, before transplanting them into their final positions, always keeping plants weed-free. Place in full sunshine to keep the bright golden foliage; too much shade, and the leaves will become greener. Use a well-drained moist soil, and add peat, leaf-mould and bonemeal to give a good start.

**Take care**
Keep plants in sun for good colour.

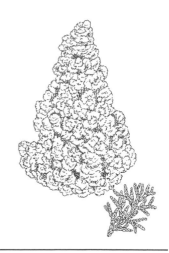

# Chamaecyparis obtusa 'Nana'

- Open site or light shade
- Well-drained garden soil
- Very slow-growing dwarf bush

Developed by the Japanese from the Hinoki cypress that grows in Japan, this is much sought after for miniature gardens and rockeries. It can take up to 100 years to reach 1.5m (5ft), and will reach only 25cm (10in) high and wide in ten years. It makes a flat-topped dome, with saucer-shaped fans of tight, dark green leaves. The green cones are borne on the branches and mature within a year.

The ripe seeds can be sown, but are unlikely to grow true. It is better to grow from cuttings. Use a half-and-half mixture of peat and sand, grow until they have rooted, and then plant out in a nursery bed. Great care is needed to prevent the plants from being choked by weeds and other plants. After three years move them to their final positions and keep a space clear around them for a few years. Use a well-drained soil that has been enriched with peat, leaf-mould and bonemeal.

**Take care**
Keep seedlings weed-free. 40♦

# Chamaecyparis obtusa 'Nana Gracilis'

- Open site or light shade
- Well-drained garden soil
- Slow-growing dwarf bush or small tree

This plant is often sold in nurseries as 'Nana', but it is larger and the sprays of foliage are much flatter. It has the same Japanese origins as 'Nana' and is very popular for the rockery or Bonsai. It will reach 1m (39in) tall and 40cm (16in) wide in ten years, with an ultimate height of about 2.4m (8ft) and a spread of 1m (39in). It is a finely formed plant with distinctive sprays of rich, dark green foliage.

The seeds can be sown and have given rise to some fine small conifers; but to be true to the parent, cuttings should be taken and pressed into a mixture of half peat and half sand. When they have rooted, plant them in nursery beds for three years; keep the ground well weeded. They can then be planted in their final situations where they can be seen to advantage, in ordinary garden soil that is moist but well-drained, with added peat, leaf-mould and bonemeal.

**Take care**
Keep seedlings weed-free. 42♦

# Chamaecyparis pisifera 'Boulevard'

- **Light shade**
- **Moist garden soil with not too much lime**
- **Quick-growing medium bush**

This cultivar was raised from Japanese parents in the 1930s, and has become very popular. It has a compact conical or pyramid shape, and the silvery steel-blue foliage is particularly strong in summer. It grows quickly, reaching 2m (6.5ft) tall by 1m (39in) wide in ten years, and can be trimmed to keep a good shape without losing its character. In 20 years it could reach 4.5m (15ft) in height, with a spread of 3m (10ft). To keep the brightness of the silvery leaves, plant it in light shade. The bush has small cones, about 6mm (0.2in) across, each with ten pointed scales.

It is very easy to strike cuttings, in a half peat and half sand mix. Plant rooted cuttings in nursery beds for three years, and then place in their final positions. The soil should be moist, and this variety will tolerate some lime; added peat, leaf-mould and bonemeal will provide nutrients for a healthy start.

**Take care**
Keep the young plants moist. 42♦

# Chamaecyparis pisifera 'Filifera Aurea'

- **Open position**
- **Moist but well-drained soil**
- **Slow-growing large shrub**

This shrub has been in cultivation for almost 100 years and was developed from plants imported from Japan. It eventually makes a shrub about 4.5m (15ft) tall, although in ten years it reaches only 1m (39in) high with a spread of 1.2m (4ft). The foliage is distinctive, like threads of gold; the branches, trailing at their tips, give the whole plant a weeping look, which is particularly effective when the plant is on a rockery with some branches trailing down over lower levels. To keep the brightness of the foliage, plant the shrub in an open position. It bears 6mm (0.2in) cones, which mature during the first year.

Propagation should be from cuttings, and it is recommended that, for a dwarfish plant with a trailing character, the cuttings should be taken from the weaker side shoots rather than the more vigorous leaders. After three years they can be planted in their final situations.

**Take care**
Keep seedlings weed-free. 42-3♦

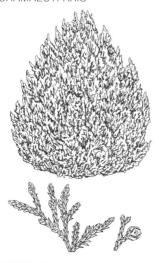
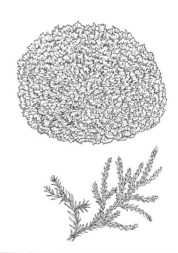

# Chamaecyparis pisifera 'Plumosa Aurea'

- Open situation
- Well-drained moist garden soil
- Fast-growing small tree

This small tree of Japanese origin is conical in shape, with densely packed branches. Its young foliage, bright yellow in colour, turns to yellow-green or bronze as it ages. The tree will grow to a height of 3m (10ft) and have a spread of 2m (6.5ft) in ten years, but it could eventually reach 8m (26ft). The leaves are coarser to touch than some plumosas, and if it has insufficient sun its gold may revert to green. The cones are 6mm (0.2in) across, and ripen in the first year.

For a plant to be true to its parent, it should be grown from cuttings. These are taken in spring, and set in half peat, half sand. When they have rooted, move them to a nursery bed for three years, then plant them in their final positions. Choose an open site with a moist but well-drained soil that has some peat, leaf-mould and bonemeal added to give the plants a good start; they should establish themselves quickly.

**Take care**
Keep young plants moist. 43♦

# Chamaecyparis pisifera 'Snow'

- Sheltered position with light shade
- Ordinary moist soil
- Slow-growing dwarf bush

This small conifer was raised in Japan, and has pale green foliage with white tips, giving the appearance of a dusting of snow over the plant. It will make a compact bush that gradually develops a more open and fern-like look. The bush reaches a height of 2m (6.5ft) if conditions are suitable; otherwise it may reach only half this size, and if given a rockery situation with a constricted root area it can be kept quite small. The cones are only 6mm (0.2in) wide, and take up to a year to ripen.

Plants should be propagated from cuttings, set into a mixture of half peat, half sand in spring. When they are rooted, move them to a nursery bed for three years, and keep the bed weeded to prevent the young plants from becoming choked. The plants can then be transplanted to their final positions, which should be in light shade and sheltered.

**Take care**
Full sunlight and cold winds can burn the foliage. 44♦

 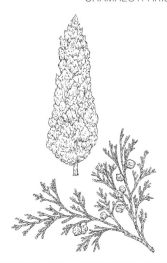

# Chamaecyparis pisifera 'Squarrosa Sulphurea'

- Open site
- Ordinary moist soil
- Small to medium bush

This cultivar, which has been grown for about 100 years, has a soft, feathery appearance. Developed from Japanese cultivars, it is ideal as a background plant or as a lawn specimen. Its golden foliage is a particularly bright sulphur-yellow when the young growth appears in spring, but by winter it has dulled down to a yellowy green tinged with bronze on the extremities. It will grow to 2m (6.5ft) tall, with a width of 1m (39in), in ten years. The cones are 6mm (0.2in) across.

Seed can be used, but for true form and colour, cuttings should be taken and set in a half peat, half sand mixture in spring. When the cuttings have rooted, plant them out into a nursery bed for three years. Then they can be placed in their final positions. Choose an open site, to keep the colour as bright as possible, with a well-drained moist soil.

These plants are usually free from pests and diseases.

**Take care**
Keep the young plants moist.

# Chamaecyparis thyoides 'Glauca'

- Open site or light shade
- Lime-free soil; can stand bog
- Small to medium tree with medium growth

The parents of this tree are native to the Eastern United States. The plant will make a conical form of small to medium size, with blue foliage. In ten years it should grow to 2m (6.5ft) tall, with an eventual height around 6m (20ft) according to the soil conditions. The foliage is in loose fans, giving it a feathery appearance; when crushed the leaves give off a pleasant scent. The cones are blue-green in colour, 6mm (0.2in) across.

The seed can be sown in trays when ripe, and only the bluest seedlings grown on for three years; then select only the best specimens for colour and form, for planting out into the final sites. Otherwise cuttings can be set in an equal mixture of peat and sand, and the rooted cuttings grown on for three years in a nursery bed, before being planted out into a moist soil. Avoid shallow chalky soils. The addition of peat, leaf-mould and bonemeal is beneficial.

**Take care**
Keep young plants moist.

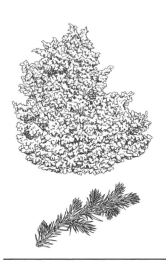
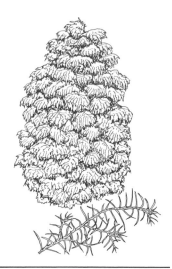

# Cryptomeria japonica 'Bandai-sugi'
- Open situation or light shade
- Moist, slightly acid soil
- Slow-growing compact bush

It is curious that this odd dwarf cultivar should have come from the large and majestic Japanese cedar. It will grow to about 1m (39in) tall and wide in ten years. A mixture of tight moss-like foliage and normal leaf growth gives it an unusual appearance. The leader growth can be strong with slight side shoots, and this, together with the leaf structure, gives it a haphazard look that some gardeners find ideal for a focal point on a rockery. The cones are just over 1.2cm (0.5in) wide, and stay on the tree for almost two years before turning brown and releasing seeds.

Propagation should be by cuttings; side shoots should be taken, to keep the cuttings less vigorous. Set in half peat, half sand until rooted, then plant out into a nursery bed for two years.

Normally this bush is pest-free, but watch for grey mould on young plants; if seen, spray with a suitable fungicide such as zineb.

**Take care**
Keep young plants moist and free from weeds. 45♦

# Cryptomeria japonica 'Elegans'
- Open or lightly shaded site
- Slightly acid, moist soil
- Small tree, grows fast at first

Brought out of Japan in 1854, this tall plant has a bushy appearance. The young soft foliage is kept throughout the plant's life, but turns from the summer blue-green to bronze or purple in winter. The tree grows quite quickly, and reaches 3m (10ft) by 1.2m (4ft) in ten years; then it slows down, to reach 12m (39ft) in about 70 years, according to the soil. There is a compact form called 'Elegans Compacta' or 'Elegans Nana'. Cones develop on the tips of the shoots, and stay on for over a year to ripen from green to brown.

Sow seeds in spring in seed compost, and move the seedlings into a nursery bed when they are 7.5cm (3in) tall. Select the best-coloured specimens only, and grow on for two or three years, then make a final selection for form and colour before planting out into their garden positions.

Normally this tree is pest-free, but watch for grey mould on seedlings, and spray with a fungicide.

**Take care**
Clear heavy snow off branches. 44-5♦

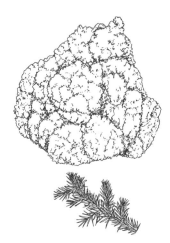

# Cryptomeria japonica 'Spiralis'
*(Granny's ringlets)*
- **Open or lightly shaded site**
- **Slightly acid, moist soil**
- **Slow-growing bush**

This plant was brought out of Japan in 1860. It normally forms a shrub about 50cm (20in) in height and width in ten years, with dense bright green leaves twisted around the branches to give a ringlet look. Sometimes, however, the plant forms a large tree, and if this occurs it can drown the surrounding planting. The cones are borne on the tips of the branches and take over a year to ripen from green to brown.

If the seed is sown, keep only the dwarf slow-growing seedlings to grow on to maturity. The best method is to grow from cuttings, using the less vigorous side shoots and setting them in a half peat, half sand mixture. When they are rooted, plant in pots for a year and then set out in nursery beds for two years. Select the best forms and plant them out in the final positions, using a deep moist soil that is slightly acid.

Usually this bush is free from pests, but spray it with a fungicide to deter grey mould.

**Take care**
Keep young plants moist. 46♦

# Cryptomeria japonica 'Vilmoriniana'
- **Open or lightly shaded site**
- **Well-drained but moist soil**
- **Slow-growing dwarf bush**

This popular dwarf bush for the rockery has little in common with its Japanese ancestors. It has very small crowded foliage on tiny branches that form into a globe. In ten years it will reach only 40cm (16in) tall with a spread of 50cm (20in); in 30 years it should grow to 60cm (24in) tall and 1m (39in) wide. The foliage is a rich green for most of the year, but turns reddish purple in winter. Cones form at the ends of the branches, and ripen the following year, turning from green to brown.

Propagate this bush from cuttings to keep plants true to type. They should be set into a half peat, half sand mixture, and the rooted cuttings put into pots for a year, then set out into nursery beds for a further year or two before being transplanted into their final situations. An open site or one with light shade is suitable.

These plants are usually free from pest attacks, but spray seedlings with fungicide to deter grey mould.

**Take care**
Keep young plants moist. 46♦

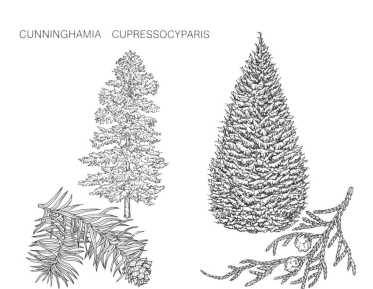

# Cunninghamia lanceolata (China fir)

- **Needs a sheltered position**
- **Ordinary well-drained soil**
- **Medium- to quick-growing small to medium tree**

This tree comes from Southern China, where it grows to a height of 25m (82ft), but in cultivation it should reach only about 4m (13ft) high and 2m (6.5ft) wide in ten years. The foliage grows down to ground level, giving the appearance of a coarse spruce; the leaves, however, are much bigger – up to 6cm (2.4in) long – and of a glossy dark green. The shape makes this tree suitable for a lawn specimen. The cones are carried on the branch tips and are about 5cm (2in) in diameter, turning from green to brown as they ripen.

The seed can be sown in a seed compost in spring, and the seedlings transplanted to a nursery bed in autumn, where they should be left for three years before planting out in their final positions. Choose an open site sheltered from strong wind, with ordinary garden soil enriched with peat, leaf-mould and bonemeal.

Normally the China fir is both pest- and disease-free.

**Take care**
Avoid a windy site. 47♦

# Cupressocyparis leylandii

*(Leyland cypress)*
- **Open situation or light shade**
- **Virtually any soil**
- **Fast-growing tree**

This hybrid between *Chamaecyparis nootkatensis* and *Cupressus macrocarpa* originated in Wales in 1888. It has a remarkable rate of growth, reaching around 4m (13ft) in six years, 15m (49ft) in 16 years, and 20m (66ft) in 30 years, with an ultimate height over 30m (98ft) depending on conditions. It forms an upright, feathery shape. It is extremely hardy, and is used extensively, though unwisely, as a hedge plant; it can easily get out of hand. The cones are about 1.2cm (0.5in) across, and ripen within the year.

Plans are best propagated from cuttings which are vigorous and easily taken. Set these into a half peat, half sand mixture in spring; in autumn the rooted cuttings can be planted in a nursery bed for a further year or two, and then put out in their final positions. This tree grows in virtually any soil, and will stand coastal air, wind and frost.

**Take care**
Leave plenty of room for growth. 48♦

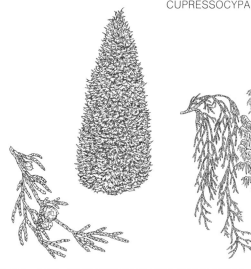

# Cupressocyparis leylandii 'Robinson's Gold'

- Open situation
- Virtually any soil
- Quick-growing tree

This golden form of the Leyland Cypress is a cross between *Chamaecyparis nootkatensis* and *Cupressus macrocarpa*. The tree is quick-growing and conical in shape, with a soft appearance due to the feathery nature of the foliage, which is borne in open fern-like sprays. The rate of growth is slower than that of the parent plants, and it makes a more compact plant. This tree should grow to 5m (16.4ft) tall in ten years, with an ultimate height of around 18m (59ft). The foliage is yellow, with a bronze-gold cast in spring. The green cones are 1.2cm (0.5in) wide.

This tree should be propagated by cuttings to retain a good colour and form. Cuttings are easy to take in spring. Set them into a mixture of half peat and half sand, and leave them till autumn. The best cuttings should then be lifted and planted into a nursery bed for a year or two, when a further selection should be made for colour and vigour.

**Take care**
Keep young plants moist.

# Cupressus cashmeriana
*(Kashmir cypress)*

- Sheltered, warm situation
- Ordinary garden soil
- Fast-growing medium tree

The origins of this tree are obscure but some authorities suggest Tibet. It makes a small to medium tree with a very graceful weeping appearance. The rate of growth is reasonably fast, and it makes a 5m (16.4ft) tall plant with a spread of 2m (6.5ft) in ten years. It forms an excellent tree for medium or large gardens, but should be screened from strong winds and bitter cold. It can be pruned to keep the shape compact without spoiling the looks and character. The foliage is grey-green, and the globe-like cones mature in their second year.

Take cuttings and grow them in pots of half peat, half sand. When they have rooted, move them to a larger pot for two years. By using pots, the plants will not have their roots disturbed unduly, and can be planted out into their final sites without trouble. This tree will grow in any but wet soils.

Watch for the cypress aphid; if it is found, spray it with malathion.

**Take care**
Place this species in a protected site.

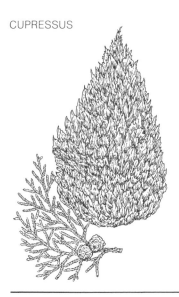

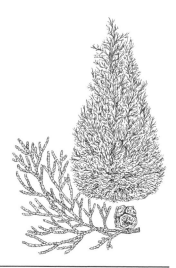

# Cupressus glabra 'Pyramidalis'

- Sunny situation
- Ordinary garden soil
- Small to medium tree with medium growth rate

This blue-foliaged conical tree has dense feathery fans of leaves, and will reach a height of 4m (13ft) with a spread of 2m (6.5ft) in ten years, with an ultimate height of 12m (39ft) depending on soil conditions. The reddish purple bark peels away in scales, leaving patches of pale yellow. The cones, over 1.2cm (0.5in) across, are purple-brown.

The plant should be propagated by cuttings taken in autumn, and set in a half peat, half sand mixture. When rooted, plant in pots of potting compost and grow on for a year. Move to their final positions in autumn. Growing in pots will prevent undue root disturbance, which they dislike. If the tree forks, prune it back to give the plant one leader. Choose a sunny position, and add peat, leaf-mould and bonemeal to the soil to give the plant a good start.

Watch for cypress aphids, and spray with malathion if the leaves turn brown and start to fall.

**Take care**
Do not disturb the roots. 65♦

# Cupressus macrocarpa 'Goldcrest'

- Sunny open situation
- Ordinary well-drained soil
- Medium-sized tree

This cultivar is regarded by some experts as the best of the golden forms. It has a narrow column-like shape and after ten years will reach 4m (13ft) in height, with a width of just over 1m (39in), and with an eventual height of about 18m (59ft) depending on soil and weather conditions. It forms a good hedge in seaside areas. The feathery foliage has scale-like bright yellow leaves in dense clusters. The cones are over 2.5cm (1in) across, and each of the 4-6 scales has a short boss.

The seed can be sown but is unlikely to breed true. It is better to grow from cuttings, which should be taken in autumn. Put them into a half peat, half sand mix until rooted, then transplant into pots with a good potting compost; make sure they have rooted and then leave them for a year. Plant out in a sheltered permanent position in ordinary soil. Spray with malathion to deter cypress aphid.

**Take care**
Protect young plants from cold. 66♦

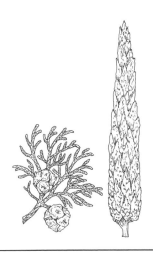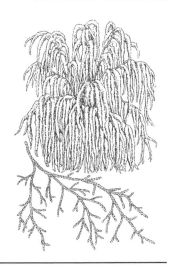

# Cupressus sempervirens
*(Italian cypress)*
- **Sunny sheltered site**
- **Ordinary well-drained soil**
- **Medium-sized tree**

This is the well-known cypress of the Mediterranean, a dark green pencil-like tree with upright branches. It will reach 3m (10ft) tall with a width of 70cm (28in) in ten years, and a height of about 15m (49ft) when mature, but in ideal conditons the tree can achieve 45m (148ft). Plant it in a sheltered warm place or the young plants may suffer cold damage.

Grow plants from cuttings as there is wide variation in seed-grown plants. Take cuttings in autumn and set in a mix of half peat and half sand until rooted, then transplant into pots of potting compost until the following autumn; plant out with the minimum of disturbance to the roots, in ordinary garden soil where there is protection from cold winds and frost. Additional peat, leaf-mould and bonemeal will improve the soil. Spray with malathion to prevent cypress aphids, and with a fungicide to stop grey mould on seedlings.

**Take care**
Avoid frost pockets.

# Dacrydium franklinii
*(Huon pine)*
- **Sheltered but warm situation**
- **Ordinary well-drained soil**
- **Large shrub with slow to medium growth rate**

This plant from Tasmania has a weeping habit. When grown in cooler areas it forms a large shrub or small conical tree reaching to just over 4.5m (15ft) with a similar spread. The bright green leaves are needle-shaped with a broad base tapering to a stiff point when young, turning to scale-like leaves as they mature. The cones are unusual, being an oval nut-like seed set into a cup.

It is possible to sow the seeds in a seed compost and grow the seedlings in pots, as they resent root movement. Cuttings can be taken but should also be grown in pots to keep the roots protected. Plant out when the plants are 30cm (12in) tall, in a warm sheltered position in an ordinary soil enriched with peat, leaf-mould and bonemeal. Screen from cold winds and frost as the plant is likely to be damaged in cold winters. Normally it is free from pest and disease attack.

**Take care**
Protect during very cold weather.

59

# Dacrydium laxifolium

*(Mountain rimu)*
- **Open position**
- **Ordinary well-drained soil**
- **Very small slow-growing prostrate shrub**

This plant from New Zealand is regarded as the smallest of all conifers, being just over 7.5cm (3in) tall. It forms a dense mat when mature, spreading to 50cm (20in) across in ten years. The plant has wiry stems, and the minute scale-like leaves turn from green to purple in winter. It will stand cold winters without undue stress. The cones are formed of a nut-like seed in a cup.

The seeds can be sown in a seed compost, and the seedlings should be kept in pots to avoid disturbing the roots. They should be planted out when a year or two old. Place in an open situation such as a rockery, in ordinary well-drained soil; the addition of peat, leaf-mould and bonemeal will help to get the plant established. Keep the young plants free from weeds and invasive plants until they are large enough to hold their own. Usually these plants are free from attacks by pests and diseases.

**Take care**
Do not disturb the root system.

# Fitzroya cupressoides

- **Open situation**
- **Well-drained garden soil**
- **Medium to large shrub or tree of slow growth**

In its native Chile and Argentina this species will grow 50m (164ft) tall and 9m (29.5ft) wide, but in cooler areas the plant will be smaller and if pruned can be kept to a bush form. The foliage consists of scale-like leaves 6mm (0.2in) long set in threes around the stems, and the extremities of the branches have a weeping effect. The cones are small, about 8mm (0.3in) across, with nine scales; they change from green to brown as they ripen, and remain on the tree through the winter, splitting to release the seed. The dark rusty brown bark peels off to show the grey trunk underneath.

The seed can be sown in a seed compost, and the seedlings put out into a sheltered nursery bed for two or three years, then transplanted into their final positions. Choose an open site with a well-drained soil enriched with peat, leaf-mould and bonemeal. These plants are normally free from attacks by pests and diseases.

**Take care**
Protect seedlings from cold until they are fully established.

# Ginkgo biloba
*(Maidenhair tree)*
- **Warm sunny position**
- **Ordinary garden soil**
- **Medium to large tree with medium rate of growth**

This curious plant grows wild in Eastern China, but fossils of its leaves have been found in various parts of the world, showing that it was widespread in prehistoric times. The ginkgo forms a medium to large tree, a 200-year-old specimen reaching over 30m (98ft), but the rate of growth is erratic, being quite rapid in hot summers but slowing down when the temperature is lower. It is one of the few conifers that is not evergreen. The flat fan-shaped yellow-green leaves turn to yellow in autumn before falling. There are male and female trees, and the cones (borne on the female plant) form a fruit enclosing an edible nut.

The ginkgo is normally grown from imported seed sown in autumn in a seed compost. Pot on when 10cm (4in) tall, and grow on for four years before planting in the final site in ordinary garden soil. Choose a warm and sunny situation.

**Take care**
Do not prune, as cut stems will die back further. 67♦

# Juniperus chinensis 'Aurea'
*(Golden Chinese juniper)*
- **Open or light shade**
- **Most garden soils**
- **Slow-growing small tree**

This yellow-foliaged cultivar is very slow-growing to start with, but quickens later to form a slender column-like tree. It will grow to 1.5m (5ft) tall and 80cm (32in) wide in ten years, and matures to about 6m (20ft) tall with a width of 1m (39in). The plant bears two types of foliage: the juvenile has needle-like leaves, and the adult ones are scale-like, which gives the plant a two-toned effect. The cones take the form of berries, and ripen in the second year, when the seeds can be extracted in autumn and sown.

To achieve a good colour and form it is better to take cuttings, setting them in a mix of half peat and half sand in a cold frame. Transplant rooted cuttings into a nursery bed for two years and then plant out into their permanent sites in ordinary soil. Some growers prefer to graft cuttings onto a healthy stock. Spray plants with malathion to prevent scale insects, and zineb to stop rust.

**Take care**
Avoid sites with too much sun. 67♦

61

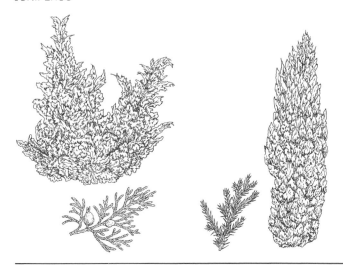

# Juniperus chinensis 'Kaizuka' *(Hollywood juniper)*

- **Any situation**
- **Most soils**
- **Large shrub with a medium rate of growth**

This has become very popular due to its upright shape, its bright green foliage and its ability to grow virtually anywhere. The branches are long and spreading, following no set pattern, and it makes a good contrast next to neat and tidy plants. It will grow to 3m (10ft) tall with a width of 1.2m (4ft) in ten years in a warm site; in cooler areas it is less vigorous. The berry-like cones take over a year to ripen.

The seed can be sown but it is better to grow plants from cuttings. These should be taken in autumn, put into a mixture of half peat and half sand, and transplanted into a nursery bed when rooted. After two years move to their permanent positions. Choose an ordinary soil, even shallow chalk, and add peat, leaf-mould and bonemeal to give a good start. To prevent scale insects spray the plant with malathion, and to stop rust infection spray with zineb.

**Take care**
Keep pruning cuts hidden behind foliage to retain appearance. 68♦

# Juniperus chinensis 'Obelisk'

- **Most situations**
- **Ordinary soil**
- **Slow-growing medium shrub**

This plant forms a narrow, slightly irregular column, with bluish green foliage that often looks paler by the exposure of the whitish undersides of the leaves. These are densely packed and needle-like. This juniper reaches a height of 3m (10ft) with a width of 80cm (32in) when fully grown, but at ten years will have reached only 1m (39in) tall. Cones are in the form of berries, which ripen in the second year.

The seed can be taken out and sown, but cuttings retain the colour and form of the parent more truly. Take cuttings in autumn, and set into a half peat and half sand mixture in a cold frame. When rooted they should be planted out into a nursery bed for two years, and then into their permanent site. Choose an ordinary soil with peat, leaf-mould and bonemeal added. The location is not critical, as they tolerate most sites. Spray with malathion and zineb to keep the plants free from pests and diseases.

**Take care**
Keep young plants free from weeds.

 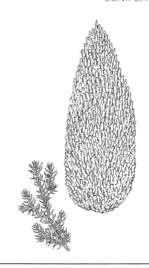

# Juniperus chinensis 'Pyramidalis'

- Grows in most positions
- Ordinary garden soil
- Slow-growing medium bush

This slow-growing conifer forms a dense cone-shaped bush that reaches 2m (6.5ft) in height and 1m (39in) wide in ten years, but when fully grown should reach nearly 5m (16.4ft) tall and 2m (6.5ft) wide. The needle-like foliage is prickly, and blue-green in colour. The rounded cones are 6mm (0.2in) wide.

The seeds can be sown in a seed compost in autumn and placed in a cold frame; plant out seedlings into nursery beds when large enough to handle. From a batch of seedlings select the best colours and forms to grow on. After two years move the plants to permanent positions. Choose a well-drained garden soil in full sun or light shade, and add peat, leaf-mould and bonemeal to assist the young plants to establish themselves quickly. Otherwise grow from cuttings set into an equal mix of peat and sand, and grow on as seedlings when rooted. Spray with malathion and zineb to keep the plants free from pests and diseases.

**Take care**
Keep young plants moist.

# Juniperus communis 'Compressa'

- Light shade or full sun
- Most soils, including chalk
- Dwarf slow-growing shrub

This cultivar of the common juniper looks like a miniature Irish yew tree, forming a tiny narrow column that reaches only 40cm (16in) tall in ten years, with a width of 10cm (4in), and has a mature height of about 80cm (32in). It grows barely 5cm (2in) a year, which makes it an ideal plant for rockeries and sink and scree gardens. The miniature needle-like foliage is dark green, and very closely set on the upright stems. The cones are small and ripen in the second year.

Propagate by taking cuttings, setting them in a half peat, half sand mixture until rooted. Transplant into pots of potting compost and grow on for two years before planting out in final positions. They tolerate most soils, including chalk, and are happy in full sun or light shade. Spray with malathion to stop attack by scale insects and red spider mite, and also with zineb to deter fungal attack.

**Take care**
Watch for red spider mites. 69●

## Juniperus communis 'Depressa Aurea'

● **Full sun**
● **Most well-drained soils**
● **Slow-growing prostrate shrub**

This is a dwarf wide-spreading bush; the branches grow just above the soil with the tips curving downwards. It reaches 1.2m (4ft) wide and 30cm (12in) tall in ten years, and an ultimate width of over 3m (10ft). This plant has needle-like leaves; in spring the young foliage is bright yellow, dulling to bronze by autumn. It makes a fine plant for a rockery or sunny border. The cones are berry-like and very small, 6mm (0.2in) wide, and turn black as they ripen during their second or even third year on the tree.

This shrub is best propagated from cuttings, which will keep the colour and habit of the parent. Set them into an equal peat and sand mixture until they have rooted, and then move to nursery beds (allowing for them to spread horizontally); after two years plant them out to their final site. Spray with malathion and zineb to keep pest and disease attack to a minimum.

**Take care**
For good colour, keep in sun. 68-9♦

## Juniperus communis 'Hibernica'

*(Irish juniper)*
● **Full sun or light shade**
● **Most garden soils**
● **Slow-growing large shrub**

This excellent narrow column-like shrub will make a fine plant for a formal arrangement. Its very upright form needs no training or trimming to keep its shape; it grows to a height of 2m (6.5ft) with a width of 40cm (16in) after ten years, and the final height is almost 6m (20ft). This is too large for the average rockery, but it is a good plant for a border or a focal point in the garden. The needle-like leaves are closely positioned on the branches. The cones are berry-like, turning black as they ripen during the second or third year.

Grow from cuttings to keep the form true. These should be set into a half peat, half sand mix; when rooted, transplant into pots or a nursery bed to grow on for two years before moving to their final situations. Choose a well-drained soil in sun or light shade. Spray the plants with malathion and zineb to keep them free from pest and disease attack.

**Take care**
Shake off excess snow, which can spread the branches. 70♦

Above: **Cupressus glabra 'Pyramidalis'**
*An attractive medium-sized tree with* *soft, dense foliage and colourful bark that peels away in scales. Grow it in ordinary soil in full sunshine.* 58♦

Above: **Ginkgo biloba**
*Known for many years from fossil
remains, this curious plant was
discovered growing wild in China.
The fresh green leaves turn yellow
and fall in the autumn, making it one
of the few deciduous conifers. 61♦*

Left: **Cupressus macrocarpa
'Goldcrest'**
*This superb variety has bright yellow
feathery foliage and a handsome
columnar shape. It forms a striking
focal point, revelling in sunshine and
a well-drained soil. 58♦*

Right: **Juniperus chinensis
'Aurea'**
*This golden juniper comes from the
Far East and is celebrated for the
combination of juvenile needle-like
and adult scale-like foliage, which
gives the plant a two-tone effect. 61♦*

Left: **Juniperus chinensis 'Kaizuka'**
*This large shrub grows in an irregular way that provides a refreshing contrast to more precise conifer shapes. It will thrive in almost any soil and position in the garden.* 62♦

Right: **Juniperus communis 'Compressa'**
*A slow-growing dwarf conifer that forms a narrow column. It is ideal for rockeries, containers and scree gardens, where its neat shape and dark colour show to advantage.* 63♦

Below: **Juniperus communis 'Depressa Aurea'**
*This prostrate variety may eventually grow to a width of about 3m (10ft), its golden-leaved shoots spreading out just above soil level.* 64♦

Above left: **Juniperus communis 'Hibernica'**
*A fine plant for formal settings, with a distinctive columnar shape and tight green needle-like foliage.* 64♦

Above: **Juniperus communis 'Hornibrookii'**
*A slow-growing spreading shrub ideal for rockeries and ground cover. It grows in sun or light shade.* 81♦

Left: **Juniperus conferta**
*This adaptable juniper will grow in most soils, including salty sand. It develops at a medium pace into a spreading prostrate shrub.* 82♦

Right: **Juniperus horizontalis 'Wiltonii'**
*A splendid dense blue conifer grown to provide good ground cover.* 82♦

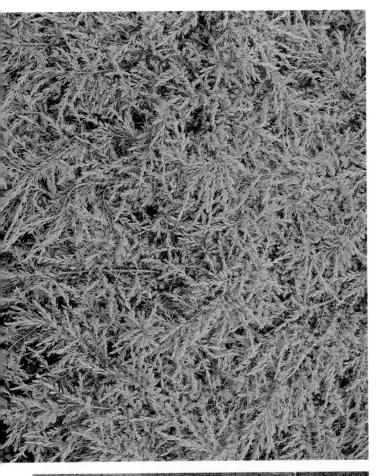

Above: **Juniperus × media 'Hetzii'**
*This medium to large shrub has
silver-blue foliage and a strong*
*shape that recommend its use in
large rockeries and borders, where it
will be in scale with other plants.* 83♦

72

Above: **Juniperus × media 'Old Gold'**
*A wide-spreading shrub that retains its superb gold colour all year.* 83♦

Below: **Juniperus × media 'Pfitzerana'**
*An extremely popular cultivar prized for its irregular spreading habit.* 84♦

Above: **Juniperus recurva coxii**
*This conifer has a weeping habit and
develops into an elegant small tree.*

*The blue-green foliage is formed in
tufts that stay on the tree for several
years before dropping.* 85♦

Above: **Juniperus sabina tamariscifolia**
*A distinctive variety with arching branches and green foliage.* 85♦

Below: **Juniperus procumbens 'Nana'**
*This dwarf prostrate shrub looks very effective on rockeries.* 84♦

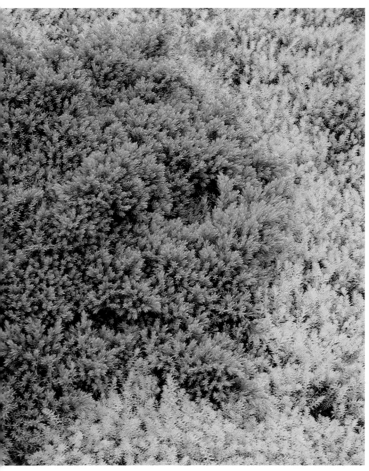

Above: **Juniperus squamata 'Blue Star'**
*Grown for its intense silver-blue colour and dwarf globe-like shape, this is a fairly new variety.* 86♦

Far left: **Juniperus scopulorum 'Grey Gleam'**
*This American cultivar develops slowly into a small tree with a narrow shape and silver-grey foliage.* 86♦

Left: **Juniperus squamata 'Meyeri'**
*Regular pruning will keep this fairly vigorous conifer in check and encourage an attractive bushy shape. It thrives in full sunshine.* 87♦

Right: **Juniperus virginiana 'Skyrocket'**
*An extremely narrow conifer that provides a vertical accent.* 88♦

Above: **Picea abies 'Little Gem'**
*This dwarf cultivar develops into an appealing compact mound of bright green foliage. Young plants should be protected from cold winds.* 91♦

Right: **Juniperus virginiana 'Grey Owl'**
*This wide-spreading shrub benefits from hard pruning to retain a good shape. The yellowish stems contrast well with the grey-green foliage.* 88♦

Below: **Larix decidua**
*This female flower will mature into a cone that gradually turns from green to brown as autumn approaches.* 89♦

Above:
**Metasequoia glyptostroboides**
This splendid fast-growing tree is
flushed with light green leaves in
spring that mature through darker
green to superb autumn shades. 90♦

## Juniperus communis 'Hornibrookii'

- Full sun or light shade
- Most garden soils
- Slow-growing dwarf spreading shrub

This plant forms a low creeping plant that follows the contours of the ground. It will spread to over 1.2m (4ft) across with a height of 25cm (10in) in the first ten years, but as it grows older it will slow down its spread and increase in height. The sharply pointed needles are grey-green with a silvery underside.

It can be grown from cuttings taken in the autumn; set them into a half peat and half sand mixture, and when rooted plant out into nursery beds with at least 20cm (8in) between the cuttings to allow for spread. Leave them to grow for two years before planting out into their permanent positions. Choose a site that is open and sunny or in light shade, with ordinary well-drained soil; add some peat, leaf-mould and bonemeal to give the plants a good start. Spray with malathion and zineb to prevent attack by red spider mites, scale insects or diseases.

**Take care**
Keep young plants weeded and moist until established. 71♦

## Juniperus communis 'Repanda'

- Full sun
- Most garden soils
- Fast-growing ground cover plant

This dwarf, densely foliaged prostrate plant will grow to a width of 2m (6.5ft) and a height of 25cm (10in) in ten years, and when fully grown forms a wide-spreading mound almost 4m (13ft) across. The leaves are needle-like but soft to the touch, green in colour during most of the year but turning bronze in winter. It has small berry-like cones that turn black when they ripen in the second or third year.

Grow from cuttings taken in autumn, and put into a mixture of half peat and half sand until rooted; transplant to a nursery bed with space for growth, keep for two years and then plant out into their final positions. Choose a sunny situation with ordinary well-drained soil, adding peat, leaf-mould and bonemeal to give good root growth. Spray with malathion to stop scale insects and red spider mite attack, and with zineb to prevent disease.

**Take care**
Keep seedlings weeded and watered until established.

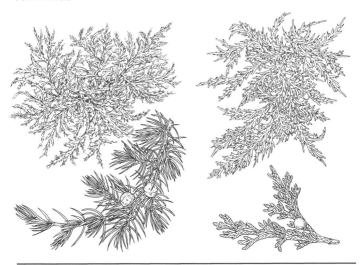

# Juniperus conferta

- **Full sun**
- **Most soils, particularly salty sands**
- **Medium-growing prostrate shrub**

This sea-shore plant forms a low-growing shrub that in ten years will spread to 2m (6.5ft) wide and a height of about 30cm (12in) in the centre, while the outer stems will hug the ground. The leaves are bright apple-green needles with a white band on the upper surface. The round cones are about 1.2cm (0.5in) across, and turn black when ripe.

Although this shrub can be grown from seed, it is usual to propagate it by cuttings; take these in autumn and set them in an equal mix of peat and sand. When they are rooted, move them to a nursery bed to grow on for two years before planting them out in their final positions. They thrive in full sun and in most soils; a good deal of sharp sand is beneficial in heavy soils and the addition of peat, leaf-mould and bonemeal will help the plant to get established. Spray with malathion to prevent attack by scale insects, and with zineb to cut down disease.

**Take care**
Keep young plants moist.

# Juniperus horizontalis 'Wiltonii'

*(Wilton carpet juniper; Blue rug)*
- **Full sun or light shade**
- **Ordinary garden soil**
- **Slow-growing prostrate shrub**

This cultivar forms a dwarf shrub with long branches that hug the ground, eventually forming a dense mat of foliage making it suitable for ground cover. It will grow to 1m (39in) across in six years, and 1.5m (5ft) in ten years, with a height of 15cm (6in). Its foliage is bright blue, and it is regarded by some experts as the best of the blue prostrate junipers; the colour turns a little deeper with cold winter temperatures. It rarely grows cones in cultivation.

It is mostly grown from cuttings, taken in autumn and set in a half-and-half mixture of peat and sand. When they have rooted, plant in pots or in a nursery bed for two years before planting out in their final positions. Grow in an open sunny site or in light shade, in ordinary garden soil; added peat, leaf-mould and bonemeal encourage good root growth. Spray with malathion and zineb to cut down attacks by pests ánd diseases.

**Take care**
Keep young plants weed-free. 71▸

# Juniperus × media 'Hetzii'

*(Hetz blue juniper)*
- **Full sun or light shade**
- **Ordinary well-drained soil**
- **Medium to large shrub**

This hybrid forms a medium to large shrub with rising branches and a silvery blue-green scale-like foliage that gives it a smooth touch. It will form a bush 2m (6.5ft) tall and as wide in ten years, and eventually about 3m (10ft) tall and wide.

It is best propagated from cuttings taken in autumn and set in a mixture of half peat and half sand; the rooted cuttings are then planted out into nursery beds, where they should stay for two years. Plant into final sites where there is full sun or light shade; the soil should be ordinary well-drained garden soil, and addition of peat, leaf-mould and bonemeal will encourage healthy root growth. To lessen the chances of scale insect attack, spray the plant with malathion. Watch for caterpillars of the juniper webber moth and treat with the same pray. Use zineb to cut down diseases.

### Take care
Keep young plants moist during drought periods. 72♦

# Juniperus × media 'Old Gold

- **Full sun**
- **Ordinary well-drained soil**
- **Slow-growing wide-spreading medium shrub**

This forms a shrub as high as it is wide, with ascending branches, giving it the look of a golden explosion. It will grow to 1.5m (5ft) wide by 70cm (28in) tall in ten years (although it can form plants of 1m (39in) wide and high in the same period), with a final size of some 2.4m (8ft) wide and 2m (6.5ft) tall. The golden scale-like leaves stay bright during winter, instead of fading like some varieties.

Grow from cuttings taken in autumn and set in a half peat and half sand mix; the rooted cuttings are then grown on in a nursery bed for two years before being planted out in their permanent situations. Select the best for colour and form. Use an open site with plenty of sun to keep a bright gold colour; an ordinary well-drained soil fortified with peat, leaf-mould and bonemeal will suit the plants well. Spray with malathion and zineb against pests and diseases.

### Take care
Keep plants in the sun for a bright gold colour. 73♦

## Juniperus × media 'Pfitzerana'
*(Pfitzer juniper)*
- Full sun or light shade
- Well-drained garden soil
- Wide-spreading medium bush

This is probably one of the most popular conifers grown. It is an excellent plant for formal or informal gardens, with its wide-spreading habit that can reach 2m (6.5ft) across by 1m (39in) high in ten years. The branches rise at an angle with a drooping tip; the whole bush has an irregular shape, with scale-like leaves of a fresh green. It is often used for covering man-holes and septic tanks, and although on the large size for the average rockery, it can be used there as a centre point around which other plants are grouped.

Grow it from cuttings taken in autumn, and set into a half peat and half sand mixture. When rooted, the best specimens should be planted out into a nursery bed for two years and then moved into their final situations. Grow in a well-drained soil, in sun or shade; peat, leaf-mould and bonemeal are helpful to the young plants.

**Take care**
Keep seedlings weed-free. 73♦

## Juniperus procumbens 'Nana'
*(Dwarf Japanese juniper)*
- Sunny position
- Well-drained garden soil
- Medium-growing dwarf shrub

This creeping plant will spread to 1.2m (4ft) across, with a centre height of 30cm (12in), to make a ground cover like a green carpet. It looks good in a rockery, is also grown for Bonsai, and can be trained to cover walls or objects. The needle-like foliage is bright green in spring, but gradually changes to blue-green as it matures. In cultivation there are no cones.

Cuttings should be taken in autumn and set into an equal mix of peat and sand. Over-winter in a cold frame, and in the following spring the best rooted cuttings can be put out into a nursery bed for two years; keep the soil free from weeds. Place in their permanent positions on a sunny site with a well-drained soil, and keep the young plants weeded. The soil can be improved with peat, leaf-mould and bonemeal, which encourage good root growth. Spray with malathion and zineb to prevent pest and disease attack.

**Take care**
Keep the young plants moist. 75♦

# Juniperus recurva coxii

*(Drooping juniper)*
- **Light shade or sun**
- **Most soils**
- **Medium-growing small tree**

This small elegant weeping tree grows to 3m (10ft) tall, with a width of 1m (39in), in ten years. In the wild it can reach 25m (82ft) but in cultivation it grows to only half this height. The needle-like leaves, spread in tufts along the branches, are blue-green in colour, turning brown as they grow old but staying on the tree for several years before dropping, and giving an appearance of poor health. The bark has a habit of hanging in papery strings. The berry-like cones, 1.2cm (0.5in) across, turn black when they ripen.

Seeds can be sown in trays, or plants grown from cuttings taken in autumn. Place cuttings in a half peat and half sand mix, keep over winter until they have rooted, and then plant out into a nursery bed for two years. Then move the young plants to their final positions in full sun or light shade, in ordinary soil. Peat, leaf-mould and bonemeal can be added.

**Take care**
Keep young plants moist until they are established. 74♦

# Juniperus sabina tamariscifolia

- **Sun or light shade**
- **Most well-drained soils**
- **Wide-spreading shrub**

This shrub has a distinctive form, with branches arching out of the centre, each branch with vertical stems spread along its length. It will grow to 1.5m (5ft) wide and 50cm (20in) tall in ten years; if conditions are right it may eventually grow to several metres wide, but it can be kept smaller by pruning. The needle-like leaves are bright green. The rounded berry-like cones are 6mm (0.2in) across.

The seeds can be sown in a seed compost; when they are large enough to handle, put them into a larger pot for a year, then move to a nursery bed for two years. Alternatively plants can be grown from cuttings set in a mixture of half peat and half sand until rooted, and then moved to a nursery bed for two years. Plant out into a well-drained soil, in sun or light shade. To give protection against pests and diseases, spray these conifers with malathion and zineb.

**Take care**
Prune to the required size. 75♦

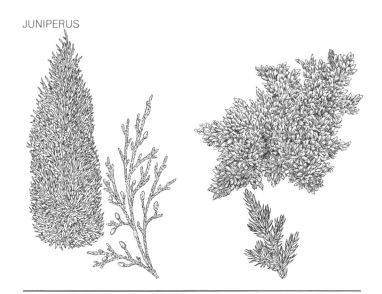

## Juniperus scopulorum 'Grey Gleam'

- Sunny position
- Well-drained soil
- Slow-growing small tree

This plant forms a narrow column that grows to about 1.2m (4ft) tall and 30cm (12in) wide in ten years. The silvery grey-blue foliage seems to become more silvery in the winter months. The leaves are scale-like, and the red-brown trunk shreds into papery strings. It is excellent for a rockery or as an accent tree in a border or lawn, and its unusual colour makes it an all-the-year focal point. The plant is male and does not bear cones.

Propagation under nursery conditions is by grafting onto a suitable stock. They are grown on as pot or container plants for several years, which accounts for their high price. Plant out into a sunny position, in a freely drained soil; the additon of peat, leaf-mould and bonemeal will encourage a good root structure. Spray with malathion and zineb to keep down pests and diseases.

**Take care**
Plant in well-drained soil. 76♦

## Juniperus squamata 'Blue Star'

- Sunny situation
- Well-drained soil
- Slow-growing dwarf bush

This new variety forms a small low shrub with quite large needle-like leaves packed on the short stems; the intense silvery blue colour gives it great impact. After ten years' growth it makes a globe 40cm (16in) in diameter; its ultimate size is still a matter for conjecture, but some experts estimate 1m (39in) tall with a slightly greater spread. The berry-like cones are just over 6mm (0.2in) wide.

Grow from cuttings taken in autumn and set into a half peat and half sand mixture. Over-winter in a cold frame, then set out in a nursery bed to grow on for two years. Plant out in final positions in a well-drained soil in full sun, keeping the young plants weeded and clear of over-shadowing plants. Give peat, leaf-mould and bonemeal to encourage good growth. To keep plants free from pest and disease attack, spray with malathion and zineb.

**Take care**
Keep young plants from being choked by larger plants. 76-7♦

## Juniperus squamata 'Meyeri'

*(Meyer juniper)*
- Full sun
- Well-drained garden soil
- Small to medium bush

This plant makes an irregular bush with arching and ascending branches that dip at the tips. It will form a bush about 2m (6.5ft) high and wide in ten years, and may eventually reach 5m (16.4ft); it can be pruned to make a more compact plant. The needle-like leaves are steel-blue in colour; then they turn brown but stay on the tree for several years before falling. The cones are like berries, 6mm (0.2in) wide.

The seeds can be sown in a seed compost but there is likely to be wide variation. It is better to grow from cuttings, taken in autumn and set into a half-and-half mix of peat and sand; keep in a cold frame over winter. Transplant the rooted cuttings into a nursery bed in spring, and grow on for two years. Plant out into permanent positions, choosing a well-drained soil enriched with peat, leaf-mould and bonemeal; to keep the blue colour, grow in a sunny place.

**Take care**
Prune hard to keep plant small. 76♦

## Juniperus virginiana 'Canaertii'

- Sun or light shade
- Most soils
- Small tree of medium growth

This cultivar forms a small dense conical tree. It will reach 3m (10ft) tall and 1m (39in) wide in ten years, with an ultimate growth of about 6m (20ft). The foliage is dark green, and a mixture of juvenile needle-like leaves and mature scale-like ones; this looks effective when dotted with the small berry-like cones, which are pale blue ripening to deep purple. The plant is hardy and will keep its green colour through the winter.

The seeds can be sown in seed compost, and seedlings selected for colour and shape. Transplant into a nursery bed when they are 7.5cm (3in) tall, and keep for two years before planting out into permanent positions. Alternatively, take cuttings in autumn, set into an equal peat and sand mix, over-winter in a cold frame and then treat as seedlings. Plant in sunshine or light shade in ordinary well-drained soil. Spray with malathion and zineb to keep pest and disease attack in check.

**Take care**
Keep young plants moist.

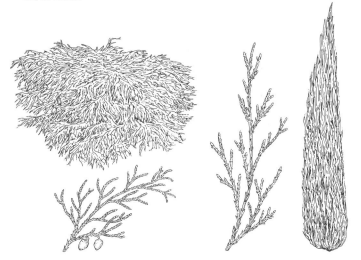

# Juniperus virginiana 'Grey Owl'
- Sunny situation
- Most soils
- Medium-growing low to medium-sized shrub

This plant has widely spreading branches of a yellow colour that contrasts well with the grey-green foliage. The plant will spread in ten years to 1.5m (5ft) wide and 45cm (18in) tall, with a dense centre but more open towards the extremities, with more pronounced thread-like stems and scale-like leaves. It is seen at its best against a dark background.

To keep a good colour and form it is best to grow new plants from cuttings. These are taken in autumn, set into a half peat and half sand mix and kept in a cold frame over winter. The rooted cuttings are then planted out into nursery beds for two years before moving to their final positions. Place them in an open sunny situation in well-drained soil enriched with peat, leaf-mould and bonemeal. Spray with malathion and zineb to prevent pests and diseases.

**Take care**
Hard pruning will keep the plant small and dense. 79♦

# Juniperus virginiana 'Skyrocket'
- Sunny position
- Well-drained garden soil
- Medium- to slow-growing small tree

This is probably the most narrow of the upright conifers in cultivation, being only 30cm (12in) wide and 2m (6.5ft) tall after ten years, and 5m (16.4ft) tall but still only 30cm (12in) wide after 20 years. It is very popular as a vertical plant for use as a contrast where there is a flat horizontal scheme, such as a heather garden or a large paved area. The scale-like foliage is a silvery blue-green.

To get the best plants, propagate from cuttings. These are taken in autumn and put into a half-and-half mixture of peat and sand. Over-winter in a cold frame, and then transplant the rooted cuttings into a nursery bed, keeping the soil well weeded. After two years move them into their final situations. Pick a sunny position with a well-drained soil, improved by digging in peat, leaf-mould and bonemeal to encourage good roots. Spray with malathion and zineb.

**Take care**
Keep young plants free of weeds. 77♦

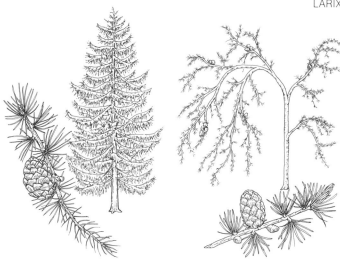

# Larix decidua
*(European larch)*
- **Open sunny position**
- **Avoid wet and shallow dry soils**
- **Fast-growing large tree**

The larch is one of the few conifers that are not evergreen; the needle-like leaves drop in autumn. It forms a tall graceful tree with a conical shape. In good conditions it can reach 42m (138ft) but it is more likely to be half this size. In 20 years it could reach 15m (49ft) tall with a spread of 6m (20ft). This is a spectacular tree; it has lovely green buds in spring, and the leaves turn a deeper green through the summer and become a rich gold in autumn before they fall. The cones vary from 1.2cm (0.5in) to 5cm (2in) long, and turn from green to brown in autumn. The bark is a warm grey with vertical cracks, and the branches droop on older trees.

Seeds can be sown in a nursery bed in spring and the seedlings moved to their final situations after two years. Plant out in an open sunny site, in ordinary moist garden soil. Spray with malathion and zineb to keep pest and disease attacks down.

**Take care**
Keep young plants free of weeds, especially grasses. 78♦

# Larix kaempferi 'Pendula'
*(Japanese larch)*
- **Open site in sun**
- **Ordinary moist garden soil**
- **Fast-growing large tree**

This form has long weeping branches, giving it a graceful appearance. It is not an evergreen, and the needle foliage drops in autumn. It will make a tall conical tree; in ten years it will reach 3m (10ft) high and 1.5m (5ft) wide. Given the right conditions it may reach a height of 30m (98ft). It can be carefully pruned to fit into a small garden, otherwise it is suitable only for the larger garden. The tree has fresh green leaves in spring, and they turn a deeper green in summer, and then to a pale buff as the leaves die. During the winter the stems have a reddish colour. The bark is a reddish brown broken into scales. The cones are 2.5cm (1in) wide and roundish, with the scales curled back like a rose.

Seeds can be sown in a nursery bed and kept for two years. The best forms (with a good weeping habit) should be selected. Plant out into ordinary soil in full sun.

**Take care**
Keep young plants moist.

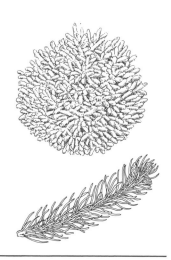

## Metasequoia glyptostroboides
*(Dawn redwood)*
- **Sun or light shade**
- **Moist soil**
- **Fast-growing large tree**

This is one of the few conifers that lose their leaves in winter. It is a medium to large tree in the wild, but has been grown in cultivation only since 1947, so it is still uncertain how big it will grow. In the wild it reaches 35m (115ft) on maturity; in ten years you can expect a height of 4m (13ft) and a spread of 2m (6.5ft). The long flat leaves are light green in spring, and turn to red and brown before falling in late autumn. The globular cones are 2.5cm (1in) across. The bark is dark grey and fissured.

So far no male flowers have appeared in cultivation. Propagation is by cuttings taken in summer and set into a half peat and half sand mixture. Put the rooted cuttings into pots, and move them into nursery beds the following autumn for two years. Plant into their final positions in a sunny place or light shade, in a moist soil. Normally this conifer is pest-and-disease-free.

**Take care**
Keep young plants watered in dry spells until fully established. 80&#9654;

## Picea abies 'Clanbrassilliana'
- **Sun or light shade, but not an exposed site**
- **Deep moist soil**
- **Slow-growing small bush**

This plant makes a low round flat-topped bush in the early stages, and matures as a dense round-topped shrub. Growth is slow; a ten-year-old plant reaches 80cm (32in) in height and spread, and it grows to a height of 1.2m (4ft) and a width of 2.4m (8ft) after 40 years. The foliage is green and becomes very noticeable in winter because of the numerous brown winter buds. Cones are about 10cm (4in) long and hang downwards; they fall in their second year.

Seeds can be sown in a seed compost, and the seedlings transplanted when 7.5cm (3in) tall into a nursery bed, where they should stay for two or three years. At this stage, select only the best plants, and move them to permanent positions. Choose an open or lightly shaded site that is not exposed to cold winds, with a deep moist soil, preferably slightly acid. This bush is ideal for rockeries and borders.

**Take care**
Keep young plants moist.

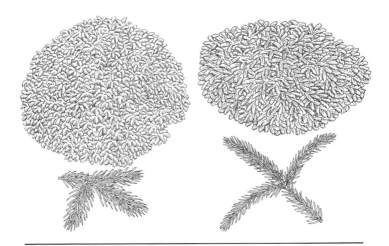

## Picea abies 'Little Gem'
- Sun or light shade
- Deep moist soil
- Slow-growing dwarf bush

This plant makes a round bun-shaped dwarf bush that is very slow-growing, reaching only about 30cm (12in) tall and wide in ten years, with a possible ultimate size of 60cm (24in) tall and a spread of 1m (39in). The leaves are small and densely packed onto the shrub. It makes an ideal subject for a rockery, or a sink or scree garden.

Seeds can be sown, but careful selection must be made to keep the form and colour of the parent. Cuttings are best taken under nursery conditions; they need to be kept in protected nursery beds for at least two years before being planted out into their final positions. Grow in an open sunny or lightly shaded site that is not exposed to cold winds. The soil should be moist and slightly acid; feed with phosphate and nitrogen in spring and summer. Spray plants with malathion and zineb to deter pests and diseases.

### Take care
Protect young plants against cold winds for best results. 78♦

## Picea abies 'Nidiformis'
- Sun or light shade
- Deep moist soil
- Slow-growing dwarf spreading bush

This cultivar makes a flat-topped dense dwarf bush with an inclination to grow outwards rather than upwards. In ten years it spreads 70cm (28in) with a height of 25cm (10in); in 20 years it has a width of 90cm (36in), and is 30cm (12in) tall. The branches rise at first as they spread, but then droop at the tips. The leaves are green, and the young growth in spring is apple-green. This plant makes a good shrub for a rockery or border, or it can be grown in a container. The cones are green and ripen to brown in autumn.

The seeds can be sown in pots, then moved to nursery rows and grown on for two years. Before planting out into their final positions, choose the best for size and colour. Plant in a deep moist soil that is slightly acid, in sun or light shade. In spring feed with a phosphate and nitrogen fertilizer. To keep plants free from pests and diseases, spray with malathion and zineb.

### Take care
Cold winds damage young plants. 9♦

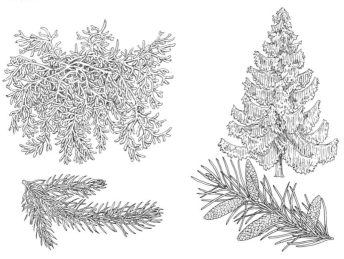

## Picea abies 'Reflexa'
*(Weeping Norway spruce)*
- Sun or light shade
- Deep moist soil
- Wide-spreading slow-growing shrub

This variety normally makes a low-growing shrub with long prostrate branches, but can be trained to form a weeping tree that makes an excellent specimen for a lawn. The rate of growth is slow – about 12.5cm (5in) a year – and a 25-year-old shrub will spread to 4m (13ft) across, with a height of 50cm (20in) in the centre. The leaves are neatly formed into furry-looking tails of mid-green. This curious plant needs a slope or large rock ledge to grow on. The cones are about 10cm (4in) long.

The seeds can be sown in pots and then transplanted to nursery beds, where they are grown for two years. Select for colour and form, and move the most weeping specimens to their permanent positions. Plant in deep moist soil, preferably slightly acid, and in sun or light shade. To keep pests and diseases at bay spray plants with malathion and zineb.

**Take care**
Cold winds damage young plants. 97♦

## Picea brewerana
*(Brewer's weeping spruce)*
- Open sun or light shade
- Deep moist soil
- Small to medium tree of medium growth rate

This very popular spruce can grow to 36m (118ft) in the wild, but in cultivation a ten-year tree will reach only 3m (10ft) high. The dark blue-green leaves are sparsely placed on the stems. The weeping habit of the stems, some of which hang almost 1m (39in) long, gives a curtain of green that looks magnificent in a large garden. The cones are 7.5cm (3in) long and ripen to brown in autumn.

It is normally propagated by seed, which is scarce and much in demand in the nursery trade. The seeds are sown in pots and grown on to specimen size. These should be planted out in a deep moist soil on the acid side, and given a feed of phosphate and nitrogen in spring and summer to supply nutrients while the tree is at its peak rate of growth. To keep the plants free from pest and disease attack, spray with malathion and zineb.

**Take care**
Keep young plants moist. 97♦

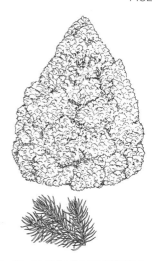

# Picea engelmannii glauca

*(Engelmann spruce)*
- **Sun or light shade**
- **Deep moist soil**
- **Small to medium tree with slow growth rate**

This plant will form a hardy pyramidal tree that in the wild reaches 30m (98ft) tall. In cultivation it makes 2m (6.5ft) high with a spread of 1.2m (4ft) in ten years, and 7.5m (25ft) tall and a width of 3m (10ft) in 20 years. The growth is dense; the blue-grey needles are soft to the touch and when crushed give off a strong scent of balsam. Cones are cylindrical, about 7.5cm (3in) long, and are brown when they ripen in autumn.

The seeds should be sown in a pot and, when 7.5cm (3in) tall, transplanted into a nursery bed for two years. Choose the best seedlings for colour and shape, and plant out on their permanent sites. Choose a deep moist soil that is slightly acid, in sun or light shade. Until they mature, give a feed of phosphate and nitrogen every spring and summer. Spray with malathion and zineb to keep pests and diseases to a minimum.

**Take care**
Keep the seedlings moist. 99♦

# Picea glauca albertiana 'Conica'

*(Dwarf Alberta spruce)*
- **Full sun or light shade**
- **Moist deep soil**
- **Slow-growing dwarf bush**

This plant makes a perfect cone shape of soft dense grass-green foliage. It will make a bush with a height of 80cm (32in) and a width of 30cm (12in) at the base in ten years; it reaches 1.2m (4ft) tall and 75cm (30in) wide in 20 years, with an ultimate height of about 3m (10ft). The plant can be trimmed to fit the available space. The cones are brown when ripe, about 2.5cm (1in) long.

The seeds should be sown in pots in spring, and put out the following year into nursery beds for two years. Choose the best forms and colours to plant out into their final positions. Select an open site in full sun or light shade, with a deep moist soil on the acid side. The young tree has a peak growth rate in spring and summer, when a feed of phosphate and nitrogen is beneficial. Spray with malathion and zineb to deter attacks by pests and diseases.

**Take care**
Water young plants in droughts. 98♦

93

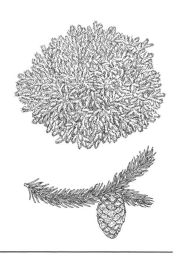

## Picea jezoensis hondoensis
*(Hondo spruce)*
- **Open sun or light shade**
- **Deep moist soil**
- **Large tree of medium growth**

This makes an upright pyramidal tree of regular shape, with an eventual height of 28m (92ft), but it makes about 3m (10ft) in height with a spread of 1.5m (5ft) in ten years. The foliage is dull green during the year but in spring the young growth emerges as light green tassels, with the young cones a rusty red colour. These cones grow to 5cm (2in) long, turning brown as they ripen in autumn.

Seeds can be sown in pots in spring and the seedlings planted out into nursery beds when 7.5cm (3in) tall. Grow on for two years and then select for a good shape and leaf colour before planting in their final positions. Grow in a deep moist soil, in full sun or light shade. Feed in spring and summer with a phosphate and nitrogen fertilizer to provide nutrition during the growing season. Spray with malathion and zineb to keep plants free from pest and disease attack.

**Take care**
Keep young plants weed-free.

## Picea mariana
*(Black spruce)*
- **Open sun or light shade**
- **Deep moist soil**
- **Medium tree of medium growth**

This medium-sized tree normally makes a height of 9m (29.5ft) in cultivation, but often reaches 30m (98ft) in the wild. As a cultivated plant it may be short-lived unless conditions are right, and it keeps a conical shape instead of the tall columnar form of its natural state. In ten years it makes a tree 2.4m (8ft) high with a width of 1.5m (5ft); in 20 years it makes a tree 4.5m (15ft) tall with a spread of 3m (10ft). The stems are densely packed on the upper surfaces with dark blue-green needles, which when crushed smell of menthol. Cones are borne in large numbers; they are 3.7cm (1.5in) long, and dark purple, turning brown.

The dwarf form 'Nana' makes a very slow-growing bun shape, 30cm (12in) tall with a spread of 60cm (24in), ideal for the rockery.

Seeds can be sown in pots and grown on for three years before planting out into a deep moist soil, in sun or light shade.

**Take care**
Keep young plants moist. 99♦

# Picea omorika
*(Serbian spruce)*
- **Open sun or light shade**
- **Moist soils**
- **Tall slender tree of medium growth**

This tall narrow tree will reach over 30m (98ft), but in ten years it should grow to 3.6m (12ft) high with a width of 2m (6.5ft); the width will increase to about 3m (10ft) and remain at this size while the height increases. Flat dark green needles are borne on branches that curve upwards. The cones are oval, 5cm (2in) long, with broad rounded scales, dark purple when young but turning brown. The reddish brown bark breaks into fine flakes and then forms plates.

Seeds can be sown in pots in spring, and grown on for three years before planting out into final positions. These trees are excellent for industrial areas because they stand pollution well. They grow in chalky soils, or in very acid peat. The dwarf variety, 'Nana', makes a small conical bush.

Feed in spring and summer with a phosphate and nitrogen fertilizer to help the plants become established. Spray with malathion and zineb.

**Take care**
Keep young plants moist.

# Picea orientalis 'Aurea'
- **Open sun**
- **Deep moist soil**
- **Medium-sized tree, slow-growing at first**

This golden-foliaged form of the Oriental spruce is slow-growing at first, but after about 15 years it increases it rate of growth unless it is planted on shallow or dry soils, where it will be short-lived. It forms a medium-sized conical tree or bush, which reaches 3m (10ft) in height and 1.2m (4ft) wide at the base in ten years, but in 20 years can reach 9m (29.5ft) in height and 4.5m (15ft) across, and ultimately 13.5m (44ft) tall in ideal conditions. The foliage is pale yellow when young, turning in summer to gold, and eventually to green. A dwarf cultivar, 'Aurea Compacta', tends to burn in hot sun but makes a fine plant for a shady location.

The seeds can be sown in spring in pots, and planted out when large enough to handle. Keep only the bright golden seedlings to grow on in nursery rows for two years. Select the best specimens and plant out into a deep moist soil, in full sun.

**Take care**
Select plants for colour and form.

## Picea pungens 'Globosa'

- Open sun or light shade
- Deep moist soil
- Small slow-growing bush

This cultivar of the Colorado spruce has a dwarf habit and forms an irregular shape, often flat-topped. It makes a bush 50cm (20in) tall and 70cm (28in) wide, with blue-grey needles. It is excellent for rockeries, sink gardens or borders. In spring the young growth appears in pale blue tufts on the ends of the branches and contrasts with the darker blue of the older leaves. The pale cones are cylindrical with pointed scales, about 10cm (4in) long, and ripen to a shiny brown.

The seeds can be sown in pots in spring; transplant the seedlings to nursery beds for two years, and keep the beds well weeded. Select the best specimens: bluer foliage and smaller plants are preferable. Plant out into deep moist soil in sun or light shade. Feed young plants with phosphate and nitrogen in spring and summer. Spray with malathion and zineb to keep down pests and diseases.

**Take care**
Water young plants in dry weather.

## Picea pungens 'Koster'

*(Koster's blue spruce)*
- Open sun
- Deep moist soil
- Small to medium tree

This is the most popular of the blue spruces, because of its intensely blue foliage, its neat habit of growth and its ability to fit into formal and informal gardens. It grows with an upright pyramidal shape to 2m (6.5ft) tall and 1m (39in) wide in ten years, with an eventual height of some 9m (29.5ft) with a spread of 3m (10ft) in good conditions. Tassels of blue leaves are enriched with pale blue tufts when new growth breaks in spring. Cones are about 10cm (4in) long, with pointed scales, and ripen to a pale brown colour.

Propagation is preferably by grafting good leader material onto a *P. pungens* stock to encourage a good upright form; this makes the plant scarce and expensive. Growing from seed gives a wide variation in both colour and form. Plant in a good deep moist soil in open sun. Spray with malathion and zineb to prevent pest and disease attack.

**Take care**
Keep young plants moist. 100♦

Above: **Picea abies 'Reflexa'**
*A wide-spreading and slow-growing shrub with a drooping habit. It can be trained to form a weeping tree.* 92♦

Below: **Picea brewerana**
*This is often regarded as the most elegant of all weeping conifers. Plant it as a fine specimen tree.* 92♦

Above: **Picea glauca albertiana 'Conica'**
*This magnificent plant develops* *slowly into a fine cone shape of densely packed foliage. It will grow to an eventual height of 3m (10ft).* 93▸

Above: **Picea mariana 'Nana'**
*This very slow-growing dwarf
cultivar forms a bun shape that is
perfect for planting on rockeries.* 94♦

Below: **Picea englemannii glauca**
*A hardy spruce cultivar that grows
slowly into a pyramidal tree. The
foliage is soft and dense.* 93♦

Above: **Picea pungens 'Koster'**
*This is one of the most popular of the blue spruces because of its intense colour, neat pyramidal form and the spectacular pale blue tufts of fresh spring growth. It will fit well into many garden situations.* 96♦

Left: **Picea pungens 'Pendula'**
*With careful training and pruning this unpredictable cultivar can be persuaded to develop a fine weeping shape. It can provide an excellent focal point in a sunny site.* 113♦

Right: **Picea pungens 'Thomsen'**
*This is another fine blue spruce suitable for the average garden. The foliage is thick and the needles long. It grows steadily into a strong upright shape and will eventually reach 9m (29.5ft) high.* 113♦

Above: **Pinus cembra**
This pine takes many years to reach maturity. It looks like a scale model of a forest tree, with a regular conical shape and thick foliage of a good green colour. It thrives in any soil in an open situation. 116♦

Left: **Pinus aristata**
A very slow-growing pine that has the distinction of being the oldest living tree species in the world. Plant it in good deep soil as a dwarf rockery plant and expect only 5cm (2in) of growth a year at most. 115♦

Right: **Pinus bungeana**
This close up shows the decorative bark, which flakes away to reveal coloured patches. The tree often branches close to the ground, a tendency to be encouraged. 116♦

Left: **Pinus densiflora 'Umbraculifera'**
*Highly prized as a container plant, this slow-growing dwarf pine produces radiating branches in the shape of an umbrella. It will bear cones as a young plant.* 118♦

Right: **Pinus leucodermis 'Compact Gem'**
*This very slow-growing pine prefers a dry, shallow chalky soil and develops into a dwarf bush of irregular conical shape with a good show of dark green foliage.* 118♦

Below: **Pinus contorta latifolia**
*Allow plenty of space for this tall tree to develop properly. It will grow steaily to a maximum height of about 25m (82ft) in cultivation. Do not plant it in chalky soils.* 117♦

Above: **Pinus montezumae**
*This tropical pine will grow perfectly well in a warm sheltered situation protected from severe frosts and cold winds. It develops into a stylish medium-sized tree.* 119♦

Left: **Pinus mugo 'Gnom'**
*This dwarf pine is in great demand for rockeries and containers, where its dense bushy shape and attractive green foliage can be seen to advantage. In spring pale young shoots stand out like 'candles'.* 119♦

Right: **Pinus mugo pumilio**
*In spring this charming dwarf conifer has a speckled appearance as fresh shoots of palest yellow-green contrast with the darker mature foliage. Highly recommended for rockeries and containers.* 120♦

Above: **Pinus parviflora**
**'Adcock's Dwarf'**
*Congested clusters of grey-green*
*needles are borne at the shoot tips of*
*this dwarf conifer. It develops slowly*
*into a compact small tree.* 121♦

Above: **Pinus nigra 'Hornibrookiana'**
*This sturdy variety will thrive in almost any situation, including windy seaside sites. It grows slowly.* 120♦

Below: **Pinus patula**
*The common name of 'weeping pine' refers to the way in which the long needles hang down from the stems of this vigorous conifer.* 121♦

Above: **Pinus pumila 'Globe'**
*The bushy form of this dwarf conifer makes it perfect for rockeries, scree gardens and containers. Avoid chalky soils for best results.* 123♦

Left: **Pinus ponderosa**
*These are the male flowers that appear in spring. Allow this densely needled pine plenty of space; it will develop into a large tree.* 122♦

Below: **Pinus pinea**
*This close up shows the orange-red bark, a decorative feature of this medium-sized tree. It will thrive in an open situation on light soils.* 122♦

Above: **Pinus strobus 'Nana'**
The long blue-green needles of this slow-growing dwarf shrub clothe the sturdy branches in attractive dense clusters. It is widely planted in rockeries and borders. 123♦

# Picea pungens 'Pendula'

- ● Open sun
- ● Deep moist soil
- ● Slow-growing small tree

This cultivar, sometimes referred to as 'Glauca Pendula', is erratic and needs careful training to give it a distinct shape. It tries to produce both leaders growing vertically and horizontal weeping branches, which makes the plant look confused, but pruning and training will make it an exciting focal point in any garden. It is difficult to give a true size for such an unpredictable plant, but it could reach 5.5m (18ft) in height and spread. The blue foliage has paler tufts of new growth on the tips in spring. The cones are 10cm (4in) long, with pointed scales, and ripen to a pale brown colour.

Propagation is by grafting to keep the true character of the parent plant; this is done by taking a cutting from the parent and grafting it onto a *P. pungens* stock. Plant in the open in a deep moist soil. To keep the plant healthy spray with malathion and zineb.

**Take care**
Train to make a good shape. 100♦

# Picea pungens 'Thomsen'

- ● Open sun
- ● Moist deep soil
- ● Small to medium tree with medium growth rate

This cultivar has a good upright habit of growth. The branches are packed with silvery-blue needles that are thicker than other forms. It makes a conical tree some 2m (6.5ft) in height and 1m (39in) wide at the base in ten years, with an ultimate height of 9m (29.5ft) and a width of 3m (10ft) in the right conditions. The spring growth forms tassels of palest silver-blue that contrasts with the older and darker foliage. Cones are 10cm (4in) long, with pointed scales, and ripen to a shiny brown. The bark is grey, and as it ages it breaks into rough plates.

Propagation is by grafting leader shoots onto a *P. pungens* stock; this ensures that the upright form and fine colour of the parent plant are maintained. Plant in the open, in a deep moist soil; a feed of phosphate and nitrogen in spring and summer is beneficial. Spray plants with malathion and zineb to keep them pest- and disease-free.

**Take care**
Keep young plants moist. 101♦

113

# Picea sitchensis
*(Sitka spruce)*
- **Sun or light shade**
- **Most soils**
- **Fast-growing large tree**

This prickly leaved spruce forms a large tree that can reach 50m (164ft) when mature; in ten years it makes a plant 10m (33ft) tall. Although too large for the average garden, it has the ability to survive moving when almost 4m (13ft) high, which makes it popular for instant planting. The foliage is green, with sharp needles; and the cones are 10cm (4in) long, green when young and turning to brown as they ripen. The bark is dark brown and makes rough plates that fall away as it ages.

Seeds can be sown in pots, and then planted out into nursery beds as seedlings, where they should stay for two years. They should then be planted out into their permanent positions in sun or light shade. They tolerate most soils, whether light sand or boggy peat. A feed of phosphate and nitrogen fertilizer in spring and summer will encourage good growth. To keep pest and disease attack to a minimum, spray plants with malathion and zineb.

**Take care**
Watch for aphid attack.

# Picea smithiana
*(Himalayan spruce)*
- **Sun or light shade**
- **Deep moist soil**
- **Large tree of medium growth**

This weeping tree makes a fine plant about 36m (118ft) tall in cultivation, but with the right conditions can make twice this height. It will reach only about 2.4 (8ft) in height and 1m (39in) wide at the base in ten years, but puts on some rapid growth to make 15m (49ft) tall and 6m (20ft) across in 20 years. The foliage is made up of green needles, and the branches have a lovely weeping habit. Young plants can be damaged by hard frosts. The cylindrical cones are 15cm (6in) long, and ripen from pale green to shiny brown; the scales become more toothed as they ripen. The bark is grey and forms circular plates as the tree ages.

Seeds can be sown in pots in spring; move the seedlings to a nursery bed when they are large enough to handle and keep them there for two years. Move them into permanent positions, choosing an open or lightly shaded site with deep moist soil.

**Take care**
Protect young plants from hard frosts; they could be damaged.

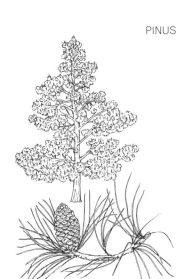

# Pinus aristata

*(Bristlecone pine)*
- **Open sun**
- **Good deep garden soil**
- **Small tree or large shrub of very slow growth**

This tree is slightly irregular in form, with upright branches densely packed with blue-green needles. It will eventually make a tree about 10m (33ft) tall but certainly not in the lifetime of the planter; it can therefore be treated as a rockery or border subject, with an average growth rate of 5cm (2in) a year. The needles are in bunches of five with paler inner surfaces. The cones are 7.5cm (3in) long, and each scale has a distinctive long bristle attached.

Seeds should be sown in pots in spring, and kept in a cold frame; plant out the seedlings the following spring into a nursery bed. Grow on for three years keeping the bed well weeded, and then plant out into final positions. Choose an open site with good soil, preferably slightly acid. Keep moist initially, but these plants are drought-resistant when established. Spray with malathion and zineb to cut down pest and disease attack.

**Take care**
Keep young plants moist. 102◆

# Pinus armandii

*(Armand's pine)*
- **Open sun**
- **Deep garden soil**
- **Medium tree of medium growth**

This plant forms an ornamental tree of medium size, with drooping leaves and decorative cones. The tree will reach a height of about 22.5m (74ft), with a spreading habit. The leaves are in bunches of five, often twisted at the base, bright green on the outside with a band of pale green on the inner side. On the mature tree, twigs are often bare for some of their length and have resinous drops on the surface. The oval cones are in groups of two or three, and about 10cm (4in) long, with thick scales, green when young and ripening to a light brown.

Seeds can be sown in spring in pots of potting compost and placed in a cold frame. The following spring, move the seedlings into a nursery bed for two years, keeping well weeded. Then transplant into final positions, which should be in good garden soil in full light. To keep plants free from pest and disease attack, sprayed them with malathion and zineb.

**Take care**
Keep young plants watered.

 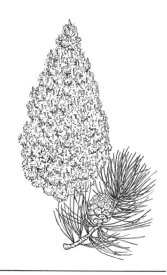

# Pinus bungeana
*(Lace-bark pine)*
- **Open sun**
- **Good garden soil**
- **Small to medium tree with medium growth rate**

This tree has unusual bark markings, and it branches quite often near the base, making a multi-stemmed tree. In the wild it can reach 30m (98ft), with a spread of 10.5m (34.5ft), but in cultivation it can be much shorter. In ten years a plant 4.5m (15ft) high with a spread of almost 3m (10ft) can be expected, depending on the way it branches near the base. Cones are over 5cm (2in) long, each scale having a short spine. The foliage is grouped into threes; the needles are often 10cm (4in) long, rigid and grey-green. The most decorative part is the smooth bark, which flakes·away leaving patches of grey, green, ochre, purple and brown.

Seeds can be sown in pots in spring, and kept in a cold frame for a year. Plant out the seedlings in nursery beds for two years. Choose an open site with ordinary garden soil. Spray the plants with malathion and zineb to keep them healthy.

**Take care**
Choose a low branching specimen to give the best effect. 103♦

# Pinus cembra
*(Arolla pine)*
- **Open situation**
- **Ordinary soil**
- **Slow-growing small to medium-sized tree**

This small tree has a conical shape, and tight clusters of short needles. The tree grows slowly reaching only 2m (6.5ft) tall in ten years, with a spread of 1m (39in); its ultimate height is about 20m (66ft). This tree has dark-green needles in groups of five, and these may stay on the tree for up to five years. The cones are deep blue, ripening to light brown; they do not open but fall to the ground, where they rot or are opened by birds or animals.

The seeds should be sown in a seed compost in pots in spring; plant out into a nursery bed the following spring and grow on for two years. The plants should be selected for a symmetrical shape and planted out in full sun in ordinary garden soil. A feed of a general fertilizer in spring will give nutrition before its growth period starts. Sprays the plants with malathion and zineb to cut down pest and disease attack.

**Take care**
Keep young plants watered in dry weather. 103♦

# Pinus contorta latifolia

*(Lodgepole pine)*
- **Open position**
- **Ordinary soil, not chalky**
- **Tall tree of medium growth**

This forms a tall conical tree that in cultivation may reach a height of 25m (82ft), but in the wild it can reach 70m (230ft). As a young plant it has a tidy habit, and its thick needled branches give it a cactus-like apearance. It will need space to grow and this should be considered when planting. A ten-year-old tree will reach 2m (6.5ft) tall, with a width of 60cm (24in). The needles are in pairs, twisted and yellow-green in colour. The cones are 5cm (2in) long, with very lightweight seed that can be blown by the wind for long distances.

The seeds can be sown in pots in spring, and the seedlings planted out the following spring into a nursery bed. The seedlings are grown on for two years and then planted in their final positions. Avoid chalky soils, but sand and poor stony ground in open sun will support these plants. A feed of a general fertilizer will encourage a good start. Spray plants with malathion and zineb.

**Take care**
Allow space for future growth. 104-5♦

# Pinus coulteri

*(Big-cone pine)*
- **Open sun**
- **Ordinary light soil**
- **Medium to large tree of fast growth rate**

This plant is notable for its enormous cones, the largest of all pines. It forms a sturdy tree with a broad open crown, and in ten years can reach a height of 7m (23ft), with an eventual height of 30m (98ft). The grey-green needles are in clusters of three, almost 35cm (14in) long. The cones are sometimes as big as 30cm (12in) long and 15cm (6in) wide, and in the green state can weigh 2.3kg (5lbs), although the tree will take up to 15 years to produce the first cones on the main stem. The cones are multi-scaled, each scale having a spine like a claw, and they remain on the tree for two years to ripen.

Seeds can be sown in pots of seed compost in spring. Keep for a year in a cold frame; and then plant out the seedlings into a nursery bed for two years. Plant out into a light soil with full sun; a feed of a general fertilizer will help good root growth. Spray the plants with malathion and zineb.

**Take care**
Avoid any falling cones when walking under mature trees.

## Pinus densiflora 'Umbraculifera'

*(Umbrella pine)*
- ● Open situation
- ● Ordinary soil
- ● Slow-growing dwarf tree

This dwarf cultivar of the Japanese red pine makes an umbrella-shaped or flat-topped tree, with branches radiating out from the trunk like umbrella ribs. The plant is very slow-growing; it reaches less than 1m (39in) in height and spread in ten years, and in 30 years it makes a tree only twice this size. These trees are prized as mature plants in containers, and command high prices for instant landscape projects. The dense foliage is a rich green, with long needles in pairs, about 7.5cm (3in) long and twisted. The small cones are produced while the plant is still young.

Seeds can be sown in pots of seed compost, kept for a year in a cold frame and then planted out into a nursery bed. After two years, transplant the seedlings into their permanent positions. Grow in ordinary soil, in full sun. Treat with malathion and zineb to deter attacks by pests and diseases.

**Take care**
Keep young plants watered. 104♦

## Pinus leucodermis 'Compact Gem'

- ● Open position
- ● Dry shallow chalk soil
- ● Slow-growing dwarf bush

This cultivar is a very slow-growing pine with upright tufts of needles in an irregular form. It will make a bush about 1.2m (4ft) tall by 1m (39in) wide in 20 years. It may have an ultimate height of 1.8m (6ft) and a spread of 1.2m (4ft), depending on soil and climatic conditions. The dark green needles are in pairs, and densely packed on the stems. Cones are dark purple, ripening to golden brown in their second year, and about 5cm (2in) long.

It is advisable to obtain grafted specimens, as seed growing results in wide variation. Grafts are taken in spring, a section of the parent plant being grafted onto a suitable stock. In this way the plant is true to its parent in form and colour. Plant in an open space, in a dry shallow chalk soil; add some moisture-retentive material such as peat or compost to give the plant a good start. An annual feed of a general fertilizer is beneficial.

**Take care**
Keep young plants well weeded. 105♦

# Pinus montezumae

*(Montezuma pine)*
- **Warm sheltered site in sunshine**
- **Ordinary soil**
- **Medium tree of medium growth**

This medium-sized conical or round-topped tree is grown for its shape, colour and large needles. Although a tropical plant, it can be grown in sheltered areas where frosts and cold winds are not too severe. It grows to 18m (59ft) eventually, but in ten years it should reach about 4m (13ft) with a spread of 1.5m (5ft). Its branches start with a drooping habit, but turn upwards at the tip. When fresh growth starts in spring, it gives a delightful effect of candles. The foliage is light blue-green, with needles up to 25cm (10in) long, in bunches of usually eight, spraying out from the stems. The cones are oval or sometimes cylindrical, up to 25cm (10in) long.

Seeds can be sown in pots in spring and kept in a cold frame until the following spring. Plant out into a sheltered nursery bed for a further two years before planting in an open warm situation with ordinary soil. Spray with malathion and zineb.

**Take care**
Choose a warm sheltered site. 106-7♦

# Pinus mugo 'Gnom'

- **Sunny site**
- **Most soils, even lime**
- **Slow-growing dwarf shrub**

This very popular dwarf shrub is much in demand for rockeries, scree gardens and containers. The plant makes a dark green bun shape, 80cm (32in) wide and 50cm (20in) tall, in ten years. It has a densely bushy structure, and the paired needles, 3.7cm (1.5in) long, are set closely on the branches. In spring the fresh growth gives the appearance of whitish candles; these pale needles gradually turn green and blend in with the previous growth. The small cones are 2.5cm (1in) long.

If the seed is sown it is unlikely to grow true. The plant is normally increased by grafting a section of the parent plant onto a rootstock of *Pinus mugo*, and in this way the dwarf character is sustained. Plant out in late autumn or (if mild) during the winter. Grow in ordinary soil – it will tolerate chalk – and place in full sun. To keep the plants healthy, spray them with malathion and zineb.

**Take care**
Keep young plants watered. 106♦

# Pinus mugo pumilio
*(Dwarf Swiss mountain pine)*
- **Full sun**
- **Most soils, even chalk**
- **Slow-growing dwarf bush**

This plant is widely used in rockeries and scree gardens, where its miniature bun shape of light yellow-green makes a focal point. It grows very slowly, making a mound 40cm (16in) across and 25cm (10in) tall in five years; in ten years it could reach 50cm (20in) across and 30cm (12in) high. The needles are closely packed in pairs on the short stems; in spring, when the fresh growth appears, the tufts of pale yellow-green give the plant a speckled look. The small cones are 2.5cm (1in) long, and turn brown when ripe.

The seed can be sown in pots. Keep in a cold frame for a year, and then make the first selection of plants for slow growth and good colour. Grow on in a nursery bed for two years, and then make a further selection to keep only the best. These are planted out in the open in ordinary soil, and will tolerate a chalky soil. Spray with malathion and zineb to deter pests and diseases.

**Take care**
Keep young plants weed-free. 107♦

# Pinus nigra 'Hornibrookiana'
- **Open position**
- **Ordinary soil**
- **Very slow-growing dwarf bush**

This plant is a dwarf cultivar of the Austrian pine, with a spreading ground-hugging character. A ten-year-old bush would be about 90cm (36in) wide and 35cm (14in) tall. The foliage is a dark rich green, prickly to the touch and grouped in pairs; it looks its best in spring when the young growth forms, first light brown buds, and then the needles emerge with a pale fresh green. The cones are small.

The seeds should not be sown, or the resulting plants will revert back in character to the large Austrian pine. It is advisable to graft a shoot from the parent plant onto a rootstock of *Pinus nigra* to keep the dwarf habit. Plant in an open position; it will grow in most soils, including chalky ones. It withstands wind and salty air, so it is suitable for seaside locations. The plants are occasionally attacked by pests and diseases, and it is wise to spray with malathion and zineb as a precaution.

**Take care**
Water young plants in droughts. 109♦

# Pinus parviflora
*(Japanese white pine)*
- **Open sun**
- **Garden soil**
- **Slow-growing small to medium tree**

This is the pine tree in the 'Willow Tree Pattern'. It forms a slow-growing bushy tree with a flat top when mature, when it should be about 10m (33ft) tall; in ten years it will reach only 1.5m (5ft) in height with a similar spread. It can be used in Bonsai. The foliage is blue-green with blue-white inner surfaces. The needles are curved, giving the plant a lively appearance; they are grouped in fives, and spread sparsely along the stem. The 5cm (2in) cones ripen from green to brown and stay on the tree for several years.

The seeds can be sown in a seed compost in pots in spring; grow on in a cold frame for a year and then plant out into a nursery bed. After two years lift the plants and move them to an open site with ordinary garden soil. Spray the plants with malathion and zineb to deter pest and disease attack.

**Take care**
Keep the young plants weeded. 108♦

# Pinus patula
*(Weeping pine)*
- **Open sheltered position**
- **Ordinary soil, not chalky**
- **Quick-growing small to medium tree**

This tree is grown for its weeping habit, due not to the shape of its branches, which grow upwards, but to the long needles that hang down like a neat fringe from the stems. The plants grow to 5m (16.4ft) tall with a width of 3m (10ft) at the base in ten years, with an eventual height of 10m (33ft) and a spread of 4.5m (15ft). The tree is susceptible to hard frost and cold winds, so protect it against the worst weather. The foliage is bright green; the needles often grow to 30cm (12in) long with a pendulous habit and are grouped in threes. The cones, often 10cm (4in) long, are borne in clusters.

The seeds can be sown in spring in pots of seed compost; grow on for a year in a cold frame before planting out into a sheltered nursery bed for two years. The plants should then be placed in a good soil that is not alkaline, where it is shady but warm and sheltered. Spray with malathion and zineb to keep plants healthy.

**Take care**
Protect from cold weather. 109♦

121

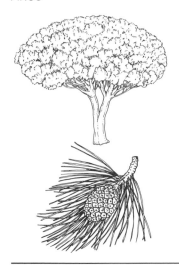

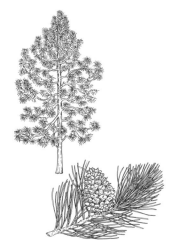

# Pinus pinea

*(Italian stone pine)*
- **Open situation**
- **Ordinary light soil**
- **Medium-growing small to medium tree**

This tree is prized for its edible seeds. Initially it forms a neat bush with blue-green leaves; but after three years it turns green, and it will eventually become a flat-topped tree with radiating branches. It grows to 3.6m (12ft) with a spread of 3m (10ft) in ten years; in 20 years it should reach twice this size, and its ultimate height is about 25m (82ft), though not in the lifetime of the planter. The pairs of needles, blue-green when the plant is young, change to green; they are 15cm (6in) long and twisted. The round green cones turn brown as they ripen, and stay on the tree for up to three years unopened. They are about 12.5cm (5in) across, and have to be in direct sunlight to open. The bark is orange-red.

   Seeds can be sown in pots in spring, placed in a cold frame for a year, then transplanted to a nursery bed for two years. Plant out in an open site in ordinary light soil. Spray with malathion and zineb to stop pest and disease attack.

**Take care**
Keep young plants moist. 111♦

# Pinus ponderosa

*(Western yellow pine)*
- **Sunny position**
- **Ordinary soil**
- **Large tree of medium growth**

This is a very variable plant due to the variety of soils, temperature and rainfall; in the best conditions it can make a tree over 60m (197ft) tall. In ten years it will reach 3m (10ft) with a width of 1.5m (5ft). The foliage is dense, as the yellow-green needles stay on for three years before falling; they are up to 25cm (10in) long, in groups of three. In spring the new shoots form candles, and open up to make a fresh green tassel or tuft. The cones are sometimes 15cm (6in) long, ripening from purple to brown, and each scale has a short bristle. The bark has scales of a warm brown colour.

   Seeds can be sown in pots of seed compost in spring, kept for a year in a cold frame, and then planted out into a nursery bed for two years. Then plant out into a sunny position in ordinary soil – the soil will determine the size, so use a shallow soil to keep the plant small. Spray with malathion and zineb to cut down attacks by pests and diseases.

**Take care**
Allow plenty of space to grow. 110♦

# Pinus pumila 'Globe'

- Sunny site
- Ordinary garden soil, not chalky
- Slow-growing dwarf bush

This cultivar from *P. pumila* forms a slow-growing dwarf plant with a bushy habit. In 20 years one can expect a plant about 60cm (24in) tall and equally wide, of densely packed brushes of blue-grey needles. The needles, up to 10cm (4in) long, are grouped in fives and the plant looks most effective when the young growth starts in spring. The cones appear while the bush is still quite young; they are oval and 5cm (2in) long.

The seed is unlikely to grow true, reverting instead to the *P. pumila* character of growth. Plants are produced in the trade by grafting cuttings taken from the parent plant onto a rootstock such as *Pinus strobus*; in this way the true form, colour and character of growth will be ensured. Place in a good light soil (but without lime) in full sun. Once established, this bush will be drought-resistant. Spray with malathion and zineb.

**Take care**
Keep young plants from being choked by weeds. 111♦

# Pinus strobus 'Nana'

*(Dwarf white pine)*
- Open position
- Ordinary soil
- Slow-growing dwarf shrub

This shrub has a very slow rate of growth and a dense compact shape, which makes it ideal for rockeries, sink or scree gardens and borders. The plant is likely to grow to 50cm (20in) tall and equally wide in ten years, and will reach about 1m (39in) high and across in 20 years. The needles are in groups of five, blue-green and up to 20cm (8in) long.

The plant is usually grown by taking a cutting of 'Nana' and grafting it onto a seedling rootstock of *P. strobus*; grown on for several years it makes a good plant, and this accounts for the high price one has to pay. There are some variations in the plants sold as 'Nana', some being more dwarf and slower growing than others. Choose a good plant with a closely packed habit, as this will be a better specimen; they are not widely stocked but are worth searching for. Plant in the open in ordinary soil. Spray with malathion and zineb to maintain health.

**Take care**
Keep young plants from being choked by larger ones. 112♦

# Pinus strobus 'Pyramidalis'

- Sunny position
- Ordinary moist soil
- Slow-growing medium tree

This plant will make a conical form to begin with, of blue-green colour, reaching 2-2.4m (6.5-8ft) with a spread of 1m (39in) in ten years. As it gets older, it takes on a pyramidal shape, with an eventual height of about 9m (29.5ft), depending on soil and climate. The foliage is made up of densely packed blue-green needles in groups of five, about 20cm (8in) long. Cones are borne on ten-year-old trees, hanging down from the branches; they are cylindrical, up to 20cm (8in) long, and have resinous beads on the scales.

The seed is not suitable for propagation. To obtain a true form it is necessary to graft a section of 'Pyramidalis' onto a rootstock of *P. strobus*; these are usually grown on under nursery conditions for up to four years to ensure a good graft. Plant in the sun, in a moist soil. Spray with malathion and zineb to prevent pests and diseases.

**Take care**
Keep young plants free from weeds.

# Pinus sylvestris

*(Scots pine)*
- Open situation
- Moist soils
- Quick-growing large tree

In good soil this tree will grow to over 30m (98ft), but on heathland and poor soil it will make only half this height. The growth is quick to start with, but gradually slows down as the tree matures. A ten-year-old tree would make a conical form almost 6m (20ft) in height with a spread of 3m (10ft). As it ages, it will develop a spreading head and a sparsely branched trunk. The foliage is blue-green, and the twisted needles, set in pairs, are usually over 5cm (2in) long. The cones, which appear after the tree is ten years old, are 5cm (2in) long, and ripen from green to brown in their second year. The bark is noticeable for its bright red-brown flaky form.

The plant is grown from seed, and grown on for three years before planting out. Generally the Scots pine is trouble-free, but spray with malathion and zineb as a precaution.

**Take care**
Beware falling dead branches. 129♦

# Pinus sylvestris 'Aurea'
- **Sunny position**
- **Ordinary soil**
- **Slow-growing small tree**

This small slow-growing tree is noticeable for its golden winter foliage. It forms a conical tree with a slightly irregular profile, growing to 2m (6.5ft) tall with a spread of 1m (39in) in ten years, and may eventually reach 6m (20ft). It is a good tree for the smaller garden, where it should not outgrow the space available. The foliage is quite densely packed when young; the new needles are blue-green in spring, taking on a yellow cast in summer, and becoming golden in winter. The needles are in pairs, about 5cm (2in) in length.

The tree should be propagated by grafting, to keep the golden quality of the foliage and the slow growth. Plant the young pines out into ordinary soil; they will not do well if the soil is dry and chalky, or damp and acid. Spray with malathion and zineb to prevent pest and disease attack.

**Take care**
Keep young plants watered in periods of dry weather. 131♦

# Pinus sylvestris 'Beuvronensis'
- **Open situation**
- **Ordinary soil**
- **Slow-growing small shrub**

This miniature Scots pine was developed from a malformation on a normal tree (called Witches' Brooms). By using one as a cutting it is possible to obtain a plant with a different growth habit. This form makes a compact dome-shaped shrub that in ten years will grow to only 60cm (24in) tall, with a spread of 1m (39in). In its early stages it is quite small and needs protection from overhanging plants. It should grow eventually to over 2m (6.5ft) tall with a width of 3m (10ft). The paired grey-green needles are about 2.5cm (1in) long, and the shrub is densely branched. The new growth in spring looks like candles.

The stock is increased by grafting, and the new plants are kept in pots for at least four years before being planted out into ordinary soil in an open situation. Sometimes the plants are kept in pots until they are large enough to face competition from other plants.

**Take care**
Keep young plants in pots for several years before planting out. 131♦

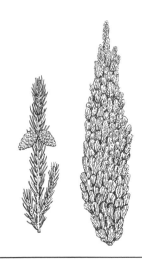

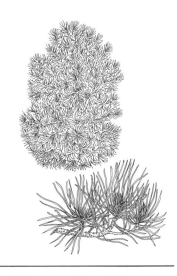

# Pinus sylvestris 'Fastigiata'

- Open situation
- Ordinary garden soil
- Slow-growing small tree

This cultivar of the Scots pine has a most unusual shape for this family, as it is very narrow for its height. Slower growing than the Scots pine, it should make a height of 2.5m (8ft) with a width of 60cm (24in) in ten years; on maturity it reaches about 10m (33ft) tall but less than 1m (39in) wide. It is one of the hardiest narrow conifers available. The foliage is blue-green; the needles grow in pairs and are about 5cm (2in) long, on closely packed upright branches. The spring growth of new leaves has the effect of candles on the branch ends.

This plant is in very short supply, due to problems of propagation, although it has been grown since the 1850s. Cuttings need to be grafted onto a rootstock and kept under nursery conditions for at least four years to ensure that the graft is good. Plant out in an ordinary soil, in full sun. The plants should be sprayed with malathion and zineb to deter pests and diseases.

**Take care**
Keep young plants well weeded. 130♦

# Pinus sylvestris 'Viridis Compacta'

- Full sun
- Ordinary soil
- Slow-growing medium shrub

This dwarf form of the Scots pine is more of a curiosity than a fine pine specimen. When young it has the appearance of a shaggy green hedgehog, but as it grows it takes on a more complex form. It reaches a rough rounded shape about 1.5m (5ft) tall with a spread of 75cm (30in) when mature, but in ten years could be expected to make 75cm (30in) in height with a width of 50cm (20in). The foliage is bright grass-green, and the 10cm (4in) twisted needles are tightly packed in pairs.

This plant is normally propagated by grafting onto a rootstock, and it is kept under nursery conditions to make sure that the union is satisfactory before being sold. The plants should be grown in an open site with ordinary garden soil. Where the soil is in doubt, add plenty of peat or compost to improve it. Spray the plants with malathion and zineb to cut down the attacks by pests and diseases.

**Take care**
In dry soils, keep the young plants moist until established. 132♦

# Pinus sylvestris 'Watereri'
- **Sunny position**
- **Ordinary soil**
- **Slow-growing small tree**

This slow-growing Socts pine has blue foliage and a rounded form. It will take many years to reach maturity; a 100-year-old specimen has reached 7.5m (25ft) tall and as wide, but for the ordinary garden it should be regarded as a dwarf plant, and should grow to 1.5m (5ft) tall with a similar spread in ten years. It has an upright growing habit that, with the blue foliage, makes it a striking plant for a rockery or border. The needles are in pairs around the stems, and in spring the tree is enhanced by the candles of young growth.

This plant should be increased by grafting cuttings onto a rootstock. Keep in a pot for several years under nursery conditions, and select only the healthiest plants. These should be planted on an open sunny site with ordinary garden soil. The addition of peat and compost will improve the plant's growth. Spray with malathion and zineb to prevent attacks by pests and diseases.

**Take care**
Keep young plants well weeded. 133♦

# Pinus wallichiana
*(Bhutan pine)*
- **Sunny position**
- **Ordinary soil**
- **Quick-growing large tree**

This plant, sometimes called *P. griffithii*, is popular as a specimen plant. Although eventually it will grow to a large tree 45m (148ft) tall, it makes a good focal point when young, as it has a fine form; but this is lost as it ages from a conical shape to a more open form. A ten-year-old tree will reach 4.3m (14ft) tall, with a width of 2m (6.5ft). It has drooping blue-grey needles in tufts of five and up to 20cm (8in) long, which set off the young shoots of upright growth in spring. The cones are 25cm (10in) long in bunches of two or three, purple-green and ripening to a rich brown in the second year.

Seeds can be sown in pots in spring, placed in a cold frame for a year, and put out into a nursery bed for two years. Then transplant them into an open and sunny position with ordinary soil; this species is not happy in shallow chalk soils but can stand some lime. A feed of a general fertilizer is beneficial.

**Take care**
Grow in the open to achieve a well-shaped specimen. 132-3♦

127

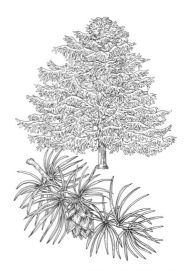

# Podocarpus andinus

*(Plum-fruited yew)*
- **Open situation**
- **Most soils**
- **Large shrub or medium tree with medium growth**

This yew-like plant forms a large shrub or medium tree depending on its environment. In the wild it grows to 15m (49ft), but in cultivation, with the right conditions, it will grow much taller in 60 years or more. The plant can be used for hedging, where it will need regular trimming and pruning. In ten years without cutting back it will reach 2.1m (7ft) with a spread of 1m (39in). The foliage is not unlike yew, with 2.5cm (1in) flat leaves, dark green on the upper side and blue-green underneath. The leaves are twisted, so the blue-green side is exposed and this gives a blue cast to the foliage. The small plum-like cones are 18mm (0.7in) long, green ripening to yellow; inside is a stone enclosing a nut, which is edible.

The seeds can be sown; grow the seedlings for two or three years in a nursery bed before planting out in a sunny situation. They thrive in most soils, alkaline or acid. Spray with malathion and zineb to keep down pest and disease attack.

**Take care**
Keep young plants watered.

# Pseudolarix amabilis

*(Golden larch)*
- **Warm sunny position**
- **Acid or neutral soil**
- **Slow-growing medium tree**

This usually forms a conical medium-sized deciduous tree, although it can reach 40m (131ft) given the right conditions, or can be contained and trained for Bonsai culture. A ten-year-old tree may reach 3m (10ft) in height with a width of 2m (6.5ft), but it will.take much longer to reach this size if the soil and climate are poor. The foliage is larch-like and light green; the 5cm (2in) needles are arranged in dense tufts in a spiral. In autumn the leaves turn a beautiful gold before falling, leaving the trunk and branches bare. This tree will withstand pollution and can grow in cities. The unusual cones look like small flowers or globe artichokes dotted along the branches.

The seeds can be sown but often fail to germinate. If sufficient seeds are sown, you may be lucky enough to obtain a few seedlings. These should be kept in pots for several years before planting out into a sheltered and sunny position, in acid or neutral soil.

**Take care**
Protect young plants in cold weather.

Above: **Pinus sylvestris**
*A close up view of the immature male
flowers of this quick-growing tree.*

*Regular in form when young, this
species matures to a more random
shape over 30m (98ft) tall.* 124♦

Left: **Pinus sylvestris 'Fastigiata'**
*This cultivar grows slowly into a tall narrow shape up to 10m (33ft) in height. It stands the cold better than other narrow conifers and will thrive in ordinary garden soil. 126*♦

Right: **Pinus sylvestris 'Aurea'**
*This attractive cultivar develops slowly into a small tree. The new needles, blue-green in spring, become tinged with yellow in summer and turn gold during the winter months. 125*♦

Below: **Pinus sylvestris 'Beuvronensis'**
*A superb miniature cultivar for borders and rockeries. The new growth forms 'candles' of fresh green above the grey-green needles of mature foliage. 125*♦

Left: **Pinus sylvestris 'Viridis Compacta'**
*This rather curious dwarf plant has long twisted needles that give it an unkempt appearance. It matures slowly into a rounded, medium-sized shrub. Grow it in full sunshine.* 126♦

Right: **Pinus sylvestris 'Watereri'**
*The upright growing habit and bluish foliage give this very slow-growing conifer a striking appearance in a heather garden or border. It will thrive in a sunny position.* 127♦

Below: **Pinus wallichiana**
*This pine forms a splendid specimen tree, especially as a young plant, when its shape is more regular than later on. The drooping blue-grey needles contrast well with the upright shoots of spring growth.* 127♦

Above: **Pseudotsuga macrocarpa**
In fertile, moist, well-drained soil this species will grow steadily to reach a maximum height of about 25m (82ft). It bears hanging cones that may grow to 18cm (7in) in length. 145♦

Above: **Pseudotsuga menziesii 'Fletcheri'**
*A popular slow-growing dwarf shrub that grows 2m (6.5ft) tall.* 145♦

Below: **Sequoia sempervirens 'Prostrata'**
*A spreading cultivar that can be trained to form a bush if desired.* 146♦

Above:
**Sequoiadendron giganteum**
*This giant among trees will grow well* *where space permits and where the* *soil is deep and moist. In ten years it* *will grow to 7.5m (25ft).* 147♦

Above: **Taxus baccata**
*A slow-growing conifer with dense dark foliage. Ideal for hedging.* 148♦

Right: **Taxus baccata**
**'Fastigiata Aurea'**
*A finely shaped golden shrub that retains its colour all the year.* 149♦

Below: **Taxus baccata**
*The poisonous seeds develop inside these red berry-like fruits.* 148♦

Above: **Taxus baccata 'Repandens'**
*A slow-growing prostrate cultivar that provides good ground cover.* 149♦

Below: **Taxus baccata 'Repens Aurea'**
*Plant this low spreading cultivar in full sun to retain its brightness.* 150♦

Above: **Taxus baccata 'Semperaurea'**
This golden cultivar will develop slowly into a medium-sized bush. The yellow colour is most intense on the new spring growth. 150♦

Above: **Thuja occidentalis 'Danica'**
This bun-shaped compact cultivar is perfect for a sunny rockery or equivalent site in a small garden. It grows slowly, its vertical sprays of bright green foliage forming a very neat and attractive shape. 151♦

Left: **Thuja occidentalis 'Rheingold'**
A splendid golden-leaved conifer that grows slowly into a large shrub. During the winter the foliage takes on an appealing copper hue. 152♦

Right: **Thuja occidentalis 'Holmstrupii'**
This magnificent cultivar develops into a pyramidal bush up to 3m (10ft) tall. The dense foliage retains a good green colour all year. 152♦

Above: **Thuja orientalis
'Aurea Nana'**
*A decorative slow-growing cultivar
that retains its compact shape.* 153♦

Below: **Thuja plicata 'Rogersii'**
*This dwarf golden conifer will suit
rockeries, heather gardens and
containers. It thrives in the sun.* 155♦

Above:
**Thuja plicata 'Stoneham Gold'**
*A compact golden cultivar extremely*
*popular for its superb yellow-tipped*
*sprays of foliage. In a sunny spot the*
*bright colour lasts all year. 156♦*

Above: **Tsuga canadensis 'Bennett'**
*This dwarf low-growing cultivar will thrive in moist well-drained soil.* 157♦

Below: **Tsuga canadensis 'Pendula'**
*A splendid medium-sized shrub with graceful weeping branches.* 158♦

# Pseudotsuga macrocarpa

*(Large-coned Douglas fir)*
- **Open situation**
- **Moist well-drained soil**
- **Medium tree of medium growth**

This tree will reach 25m (82ft) where conditions are good, but can be dwarfed to 9m (29.5ft) if the roots are constricted and there is a lack of nutrition. The tree should make 4.5m (15ft) in growth in the first ten years, with a spread of just over 2m (6.5ft). The needle-like foliage is 2.5cm (1in) long, narrow, green and slightly curved. The cones are up to 18cm (7in) long and hang downwards. The bark is grey with wide brown vertical fissures.

The seed should be sown in pots in spring, kept in a cold frame and, when the seedlings are large enough to handle, moved to a nursery bed for two years. Transplant out into their permanent positions where there is a deep moist but well-drained soil that is not chalky. An area of high rainfall is excellent. Keep the ground around the young plants free from weeds. Spray with malathion and zineb to deter pests and diseases.

**Take care**
Keep young plants well weeded. 134♦

# Pseudotsuga menziesii 'Fletcheri'

- **Open position**
- **Deep moist well-drained soil**
- **Slow-growing dwarf shrub**

This plant is also called *P. glauca 'Fletcheri'*. It forms an irregular round bush with a flat top and may eventually reach 2m (6.5ft) high and wide. In ten years a plant 35cm (14in) tall and with a similar spread can be expected; it will reach 60cm (24in) in both height and width in 20 years. This size makes it ideal for a rockery or border, where it can grow undisturbed for years. The dense foliage is arranged on each side of the branch, with short blue-green needles; in spring the plant has a spotted effect because of the pale buds opening on the branch ends. It can be pruned to shape.

This tree rarely produces cones; propagate by either cuttings or grafting. The young plant should be kept under nursery conditions for several years to ensure that the graft is satisfactory or the cutting healthy. Plant in an open position with a moist well-drained soil, preferably acid or neutral.

**Take care**
Keep young plants watered. 135♦

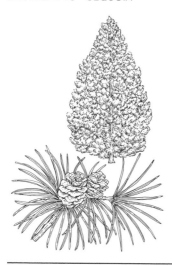

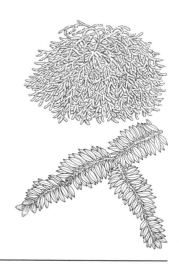

# Sciadopitys verticillata

*(Japanese umbrella tree)*
- Partial shade
- Lime-free soil
- Eventually forms a large tree

This Japanese plant derives its common name from the whorls of green needles on the stem ends, which radiate out like ribs on an umbrella. It is very slow-growing to start with: in the first ten years it will grow only about 50cm (20in) tall and 40cm (16in) wide, but then it increases its rate of growth to make a conical tree, in cultivation, of 18m (59ft) tall and 9m (29.5ft) wide at the base, though in the wild it can reach 45m (148ft). The foliage is glossy green, with needles up to 12.5cm (5in) long, and the cones are green turning to brown over two years.

The seeds can be sown in pots in spring, and kept in a cold frame for a year; then plant out into a nursery bed, keeping the young seedlings weeded. After two years they can be moved to their permanent positions. Choose a site that is partially shaded, and with a lime-free soil. To keep down attacks by pests and diseases spray with malathion and zineb.

## Take care
Keep young plants weed-free.

# Sequoia sempervirens 'Prostrata'

- Open position or light shade
- Ordinary moist soil
- Slow-growing dwarf shrub

This is a cultivar of the world's tallest tree, but in size bears no resemblance to it. It tends to grow sideways rather than upwards, to form a slow-growing dwarf bush thickly covered in blue-green leaves. The plant should reach 10cm (4in) tall with a spread of 60cm (24in) in ten years, if encouraged to grow as a prostrate plant; but it can be trained to form a bush with more height than spread. The eventual size is unknown, as it has been in cultivation for only 30 years. The foliage is densely packed on the stems in two ranks of scale-like leaves.

The plants are grown from cuttings taken in autumn; set them in a half peat, half sand mixture, and place in a cold frame until spring. Move rooted cuttings to a nursery bed for two years, then plant out into their permanent positions. They will grow in shade but perform better in the open. Normally they are trouble free.

## Take care
Young plants are prone to frost damage on the stem tips. 135♦

# Sequoiadendron giganteum

*(Big tree; Wellingtonia)*
- **Open situation**
- **Deep moist soil**
- **Very large tree**

This is a giant among trees; although not the tallest, it is the largest, one specimen in California having a height of 100m (328ft) and a girth at 1.5m (5ft) of 24m (79ft), with an estimated age of 2,000 years. To achieve this size the soil has to be deep and rich, with a rainfall of 127cm (50in) a year. In a garden, a ten-year-old tree would be about 7.5m (25ft) tall and 3.6m (12ft) wide, with a densely branched conical shape. In 20 years it would grow to 15m (49ft) high with a 6m (20ft) spread. The scale-like foliage is bright green. The green cones are 7.5cm (3in) long, and ripen to brown; they are rarely borne before the tree is 30 years old.

Seeds can be sown in pots in spring, and kept in a cold frame for a year. The seedlings are then planted out into nursery beds for two years. Plant out in an open place with a deep moist soil. This species is only suitable for large gardens and parks.

**Take care**
Keep young plants watered. 136♦

# Taxodium ascendens 'Nutans'

- **Open site or partial shade**
- **Lime-free wet soil**
- **Small to medium tree**

'Nutans' makes an irregular column-like tree of small to medium size that loses its leaves in winter. It should grow to a height of 3.6m (12ft) with a spread of 1.8m (6ft) in ten years, and have an eventual height of 9m (29.5ft). The foliage consists of small, scale-like leaves closely set on shoots that stand up when young but gradually curl over, turning to golden-brown in autumn, when they fall complete with the stem. The cones are 2.5cm (1in) across, like rough balls, and turn from purple-green to brown as they ripen.

The seeds can be sown in moist compost in spring and kept in a cold frame for a year. Plant out into a nursery bed for two or three years and then place in permanent positions in spring. Choose a wet or very moist soil, in sun or partial shade. Keep the young plants moist in dry weather, and protect them in cold and frosty areas to prevent damage to young shoots.

**Take care**
Prevent frost damage.

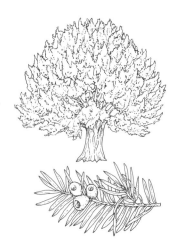

# Taxodium distichum
*(Swamp cypress; Bald cypress)*
- **Sheltered position in sun or partial shade**
- **Wet or moist soil**
- **Large tree of moderate growth**

The best conifer for swampy conditions, this species makes a broad conical shape that can reach 45m (148ft) in the wild. In cultivation, it should reach 5m (16.4ft) tall with a width of 2.4m (8ft) in 10 years, 10.5m (34.5ft) tall with a width of 4.5m (15ft) in 20 years. Branchlets hang off the branches, and have a row of small needle-like leaves down each side. The leaves are bright green in spring and summer, turning a rich ochre in autumn, and they fall complete with the branchlet. The ball-shaped cones are green, ripening to purple-brown. The spectacular root formation spreads out from the trunk in a ridge, disappearing under ground and reappearing on wet sites as 'knee-like' growths.

These plants can be grown from seeds, which should be sown in pots in spring, kept in a cold frame for a year, and then planted out into a nursery bed. After two years transfer the plants to a wet or moist soil.

**Take care**
Protect against hard frosts.

# Taxus baccata
*(English yew; Common yew)*
- **Sun or shade**
- **Well-drained soil**
- **Slow-growing small to medium-sized tree**

The leaves and seeds of this tree are poisonous if eaten by human beings (especially children) or many animals. The tree forms a rounded shape and its dark green colour makes it an excellent background hedge plant. As a tree it can grow to 25m (82ft) tall, with a wide spreading habit. In ten years it should reach 2.1m (7ft) with a similar spread; in 20 years it should be 4.5m (15ft) tall and equally wide. The black-green flat leaves are packed into two ranks on the stalks, which gives the plant its dense appearance. The berry-like cones are red when ripe.

The seeds should be sown in spring; they can be kept in a cold frame for a year, but grow quite well in the open soil. The seedlings should then have two years in a nursery bed before being planted into final positions. Use a well-drained soil, acid or alkaline, in sun or shade. They take to pruning and shaping quite happily.

**Take care**
This plant is poisonous. 137♦

# Taxus baccata 'Fastigiata Aurea'
*((Golden Irish yew)*
- **Open site**
- **Well-drained soil**
- **Slow-growing large shrub**

This shrub has a very neat upright form, and golden leaves. It forms a narrow bowl shape with very tight foliage, which gives it a solid look. A ten-year-old plant will reach 2m (6.5ft) tall with a spread of 65cm (26in), and it will eventually reach 4.9m (16ft) high. The foliage is a glorious yellow-gold, holding its colour right through the winter.

Propagate by cuttings in autumn; set them in a half-and-half mixture of peat and sand, and in the following spring move the rooted cuttings to a nursery bed. Grow on for two years and then plant out into their final positions. Choose a soil that is well-drained, either acid or alkaline, and in full sun to encourage a good gold colour. If using them for a hedge, plant at least 35cm (14in) apart; a feed of a general fertilizer will give them a good start. Spray with malathion to deter pests.

**Take care**
This plant is poisonous. 137♦

# Taxus baccata 'Repandens'
- **Sun or shade**
- **Well-drained soil**
- **Low, slow-growing shrub**

This makes a low wide-spreading bush, excellent as a ground cover plant. It is slow-growing, reaching 40cm (16in) tall and 1.5m (5ft) wide in ten years, and with an ultimate height of 1m (39in) and a spread of 4m (13ft). The foliage is dense and tidy, with dark green leaves packed along the stems; the branches spread with a characteristic droop at the tips. This is a female shrub, and the berry-like cones turn bright red.

The seeds can be sown, but seedlings are unlikely to grow true. Take cuttings in autumn, set in a half peat and half sand mix, keep in a cold frame over winter, and plant out the rooted cuttings into a nursery bed in spring. After two years plant out into their final situations. Most well-drained soils are suitable, and the plant thrives in full sun or shade. Plant this shrub where children and animals cannot eat the leaves or berries, as it is poisonous. Spray with malathion to keep pest-free.

**Take care**
This plant is poisonus. 138♦

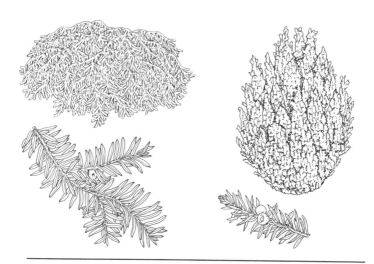

## Taxus baccata 'Repens Aurea'

- Full sun
- Well-drained soil
- Slow-growing ground cover

This is similar in habit to *Taxus baccata* 'Repandens', but it also has variegated leaves. It grows slowly, to make a plant 35cm (14in) high with a width of 1m (39in) in ten years; over the years it reaches about 3m (10ft) wide and 90cm (36in) tall. The spreading branches can be trimmed back to a domed shape. The foliage is dense, and each leaf is green with a margin of gold – pale gold in spring but gradually becoming deeper. The branches spread, with drooping tips.

Grow from cuttings taken in autumn, struck in a half peat and half sand mixture and over-wintered in a cold frame. In spring set the rooted cuttings in a nursery bed for two years. The plants should be placed in well-drained soil in full sun; shade would make the plant lose its golden colour and revert to green. This plant is poisonous so only grow it in an area without children or animals. To protect the plant from pest attack, spray it with malathion.

**Take care**
This plant is poisonous. 138♦

## Taxus baccata 'Semperaurea'

*(Evergold English yew)*
- Full sun
- Well-drained soil
- Slow-growing medium shrub

This golden-foliaged shrub makes a bush that is rather irregular in shape with upright branches densely packed with foliage. It grows 1m (39in) in height and width in ten years, and ultimately reaches 3m (10ft) tall and equally wide. The foliage is golden when freshly opened in spring, gradually becoming more browny-yellow through the year. The shape of the plant can be controlled by pruning or clipping.

The plant has no cones, as it is a male form, and has to be propagated by cuttings. These should be taken in autumn, set in a half-and-half mix of peat and sand, and over-wintered in a cold frame. In spring transplant the rooted cuttings into nursery beds for two years. Then move them to permanent positions in a well-drained soil, and in full sun to keep the gold colour of the foliage. Spray with malathion to keep the plants free from pests.

**Take care**
This plant is poisonous. 139♦

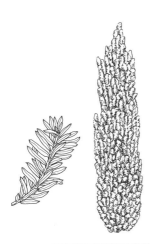
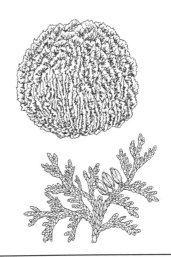

# Taxus baccata 'Standishii'

- Open sun
- Well-drained soil
- Slow-growing medium shrub

This is a narrow upright form with golden foliage, and very slow growing. It makes an ideal subject for a rockery, container or scree garden. It is a cultivar of the Irish yew, with the same neat character and tight foliage. In ten years it could reach 70cm (28in) tall with a spread of 15cm (6in), and its final size is just over 1.5m (5ft). The foliage is a beautiful gold, especially in winter, and closely hugs the upright branches, which lie tight to the central stem; the leaves radiate from the stem. Cones are borne as berries that ripen to a bright red.

To keep the character, this plant has to be propagated by cuttings, which should be taken in autumn, struck in a half peat and half sand mixture and grown in a cold frame over winter. Set out the rooted cuttings into a nursery bed in spring, and after two years move them to their final positions in well-drained soil in full sun to keep the colour.

**Take care**
This plant is poisonous.

# Thuja occidentalis 'Danica'

- Full sun
- Deep moist soil
- Slow-growing dwarf bush

This cultivar forms a small slow-growing bun that looks fine on a rockery or among heathers. It will grow to 30cm (12in) tall with a spread of 45cm (18in) in ten years, and eventually reaches about 75cm (30in) high and 1.2m (4ft) wide. The scale-like foliage is carried on fans in vertical sprays, which gives it a very neat shape. The bright green leaf colour turns bronze during the winter months, and if crushed the leaves give off an apple-like scent. Cones are yellow-green, ripening to brown in autumn, and about 1.25cm (0.5in) across.

To obtain plants with the characteristics of the parent, take cuttings in autumn, set in a mixture of half peat and half sand, and keep in a cold frame during the winter. Put rooted cuttings into pots of potting compost and plunge out of doors into a nursery bed for two years. Plant out in a sheltered position in full sun in a deep moist soil.

**Take care**
Keep young plants moist. 140-1▸

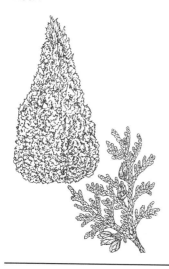
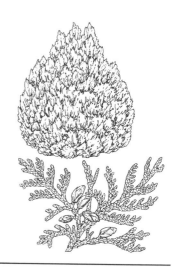

# Thuja occidentalis 'Holmstrupii'
- ● **Full sun in sheltered position**
- ● **Deep moist soil**
- ● **Slow-growing medium bush**

This cultivar forms a pyramidal bush that grows well in a border or rockery. At ten years old the plant will be about 1.5m (5ft) tall with a width of 60cm (24in) across the base, and its ultimate height is around 3m (10ft). This slow-growing shrub has bright yellow-green foliage in closely packed fans of scale-like leaves. The leaves bronze slightly during the winter in cold areas, but this cultivar is one of the best to keep a good green colour. The cones are green, ripening to brown, and about 2.5cm (1in) across.

The plants can be grown from cuttings taken in autumn, set into a half peat and half sand mixture, and kept in a cold frame over winter. Then put the rooted cuttings into pots and plunge these into a nursery bed for two years. After this period transplant them into deep moist soil in a sheltered position in full sun. A spring feed of a general fertilizer and a mulch of peat and compost will keep the plants growing well.

**Take care**
Keep young plants weed-free. 141▶

# Thuja occidentalis 'Rheingold'
- ● **Full sun**
- ● **Deep moist soil**
- ● **Slow-growing large shrub**

Regarded by some experts as one of the best golden leaved conifers, 'Rheingold' will make a low-growing shrub, with a flattened cone shape wider than it is tall, and of a fine gold colour. In ten years it will reach about 70cm (28in) tall with a spread of 1.2m (4ft), with an eventual size of almost 4m (13ft) across. This plant fits in well with heathers or on a large rockery. The foliage is densely formed of loose fans of golden scale-like leaves that smell fruity when crushed. During the winter, the gold darkens to copper. The plant can be trimmed to shape. Cones are 2.5cm (1in) wide, and ripen from green to brown.

The plant is propagated from cuttings taken in autumn and put into a half peat, half sand mixture, kept in a cold frame until spring, and then potted. The pots are plunged into a nursery bed for two years. Then plant out into their final positions, in full sun and a deep moist soil. Usually these plants are trouble-free.

**Take care**
Keep young plants watered. 140▶

 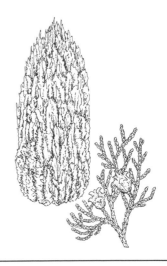

# Thuja orientalis 'Aurea Nana'
- Full sun
- Deep moist soil
- Slow-growing small shrub

'Aurea Nana' makes a rounded cone shape of yellow-green that fits in with rockeries, borders, scree or heather gardens. It is a dwarf conifer growing to 60cm (24in) tall with a spread of 50cm (20in) in ten years, and it rarely reaches higher than 1m (39in). The foliage is in vertical fans of densely packed scale-like leaves of yellow-green, which turn gold in winter. It hardly ever needs trimming. The small cones are about 1.8cm (0.7in) wide, ripening from green to brown in autumn, and have six hooked scales.

This plant is increased by cuttings. Take these in autumn, set into a half-and-half mixture of peat and sand, and over-winter in a cold frame. The rooted seedlings should be potted and sunk into a nursery bed for two years. Put out the plants into their final positions, choosing a deep moist soil in full sun. Generally this shrub is trouble-free.

**Take care**
Plant in full sun for good colour. 142♦

# Thuja orientalis 'Conspicua'
- Open sunny position
- Deep moist soil
- Quick-growing medium shrub

This quick-growing cultivar makes a medium to large shrub of conical upright shape, with golden-yellow foliage. At ten years it will have reached almost 2m (6.5ft) tall with a spread of 1m (39in) across the base; a 20-year-old plant will be over 2.4m (8ft), and its ultimate height is about 3.6m (12ft) with a spread of 1.5m (5ft). The size makes this plant unsuitable for small rockeries but it is excellent in borders and heather gardens. The foliage is in dense vertical sprays of scale-like golden-yellow leaves. The small cones are 1.8cm (0.7in) across, green ripening to brown in autumn, with six hooked scales.

The plant is propagated from cuttings. Take these in autumn, set into a half peat and half sand mix, and over-winter in a cold frame. Set out the rooted cuttings into a nursery bed for two years, and then move them to permanent positions in deep moist soil in full sunshine. The plant is normally trouble-free.

**Take care**
Keep young plants moist.

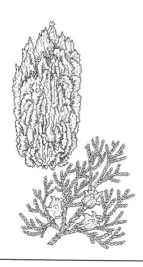

# Thuja orientalis 'Elegantissima'

- Full sun
- Deep moist soil
- Medium-sized shrub

This cultivar has golden tips to its green foliage; a good specimen looks like a golden conifer in summer, but turns green or bronze in winter. It forms a conical column about 1.5m (5ft) tall, with a spread of 75cm (30in), in ten years, and will mature into a shrub 4m (13ft) tall, with a spread of 1.8m (6ft). The sprays of scale-like leaves are held vertically. The colour is brighter if it is grown in full sunshine; in cold areas the foliage will brown in winter, but with some protection it should keep a good green colour. The cones are 1.8cm (0.7in) wide and formed of six hooked scales.

Grow these plants from cuttings taken in autumn; set into a half peat, half sand mixture to root, and keep in a cold frame until spring. The rooted cuttings should be moved into a nursery bed to grow on for two years, and then transplanted to their final positions. Grow in a deep moist soil in full sunshine.

**Take care**
Choose a sheltered position for good colour during the winter months.

# Thuja plicata

*(Western red cedar)*

- Sunshine or shade
- Most soils
- Fast-growing large tree

This large conical tree has rich, glossy green foliage. It is ideal as a specimen in a large lawn or park, but is not recommended for a small garden. The tree will eventually grow 40m (131ft) tall with a spread of 18m (59ft); but in ten years it makes a tree 4m (13ft) tall and 2.4m (8ft) wide. The scale-like foliage is in large sprays, often drooping, and emitting a fruity scent. It stands trimming and pruning, and can be treated as a large hedge plant. The cones are about 1.25cm (0.5in) wide, with up to 12 scales, and ripen from green to brown in autumn.

The seeds can be sown in late winter. When seedlings are 7.5cm (3in) tall, transplant into nursery beds for two years. Move into final situations, in a deep moist soil in sun or shade. They will grow happily in shallow chalk soils. If grown as a hedge, plant 45cm (18in) apart and keep the ground clear of weeds until established. These plants are usually free from pests and diseases.

**Take care**
Keep young plants moist.

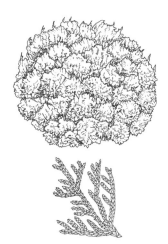
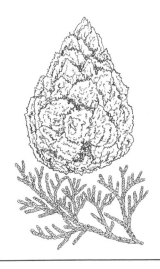

# Thuja plicata 'Hillieri'
- Sunshine or shade
- Deep moist soil
- Slow-growing medium bush

This plant is noted for its dwarf form, very slow rate of growth and moss-like foliage. In ten years it will reach 1m (39in) tall and equally wide; in 20 years it will reach 2m (6.5ft) tall and wide, making an irregular ball of bright green foliage. The dwarf foliage is of tiny scale-like leaves carried in dense clusters on thick rigid branches. Vertical leaders shoot up about 10cm (4in), and if these begin to dominate the shrub they should be cut off.

Cuttings of the dwarf-type tips should be taken in autumn and set into a half peat and half sand mix; keep in a cold frame until spring, then set out the rooted cuttings in a nursery bed. After two years growth, move the plants to their final positions. Grow in a deep moist soil, in sun or in shade. Keep the plants well weeded until they are established. Generally this bush is trouble-free.

**Take care**
Weed young plants, and water them in dry weather.

# Thuja plicata 'Rogersii'
- Sunny position
- Deep moist soil
- Slow-growing dwarf shrub

This dwarf plant has a fine conical shape and golden foliage, and is ideal for rockeries, scree or heather gardens or containers. In ten years this slow-growing plant will reach 70cm (28in) high with a spread of 40cm (16in), and in 30 years it can grow over 1m (39in) tall and almost as wide, but careful pruning will make a columnar form or wide-spreading bun shape. The fine foliage is densely packed in tight clusters, green in colour, with the edges of the scale-like leaf fans gold, and in winter this turns to bronze. Keep it in full sunlight to retain the gold.

Propagation is by cuttings, taken in autumn. Set in a half-and-half mixture of peat and sand, and over-winter in a cold frame. In spring pot the rooted cuttings and plunge them into a nursery bed for two years. They can then be planted out into permanent positions in full sun and a deep moist soil. These plants are trouble-free.

**Take care**
Water young plants in droughts. 142♦

155

# Thuja plicata 'Stoneham Gold'
- Full sunlight
- Deep moist soil
- Slow-growing small shrub

This plant's rich golden-yellow foliage is as bright in winter as in summer. In ten years this compact plant will have reached just over 70cm (28in) tall and 35cm (14in) wide; its ultimate size is estimated at just over 2m (6.5ft). The foliage is dark green in the depths of the closely packed scale-like leaf sprays, but on the outer edges the colour pales to a bright orange-yellow. It can be trained to form a definite cone or ball shape.

The plant is grown from cuttings taken in autumn and set in a mixture of peat and sand. Keep these in a cold frame during the winter and pot up the rooted cuttings in spring. Place in a nursery bed for two years and then plant out in full sun in a deep moist soil. These plants are usually free from pest and disease attack.

**Take care**
In dry weather, keep young plants watered until established. 143♦

# Torreya californica
*(Californian nutmeg)*
- Sunlight or shade
- Chalky soil
- Small to medium-sized slow-growing tree

This tree has a conical shape, with branches down to the ground, and a yew-like appearance. In the wild grows to 21m (69ft) or more, but in cultivation it is much smaller, and should reach 2.4m (8ft) in ten years with a spread of 1.2m (4ft). The 7.5cm (3in) long flat leaves, with a sharp spine at the end, are a dark yellowish green on the upper side and have two pale stripes on the underside. The fruit-like cones are 3.7cm (1.5in) long, green, and ripen with purple streaks.

The seeds can be sown in spring in pots of seed compost, and grown for a year in a cold frame. The seedlings should then be put out into a nursery bed for two years before being moved to their final situations. Keep the young plants weeded, and watered in dry weather. They will grow in chalky soils and tolerate shade, but most garden soils and positions would be satisfactory. Spray with malathion and zineb.

**Take care**
Keep young plants weeded.

# Tsuga canadensis 'Bennett'

- **Partial shade**
- **Moist well-drained soil**
- **Slow-growing dwarf shrub**

This plant is dwarf in character, making a low spreading plant with small yew-like leaves. It will grow slowly to just over 30cm (12in) tall with a spread of 60cm (24in) in ten years, and eventually makes a shrub about 1.2 (4ft) high and 2.4m (8ft) wide. The foliage is a fresh mid-green. The flat leaves are about 1.25cm (0.5in) long, set in rows on either side and on top of the stem; these are crowded together to form a tight bush, with the branch tips slightly drooping.

The plant is propagated by cuttings in autumn; set them in a half-and-half mixture of peat and sand and over-winter in a cold frame. In spring put the rooted cuttings into pots and plunge them into a nursery bed for three years. Keep the bed clear of weeds, and water the young plants in dry weather. Plant out into a moist well-drained soil in partial shade, sheltered from dry winds. Normally this shrub is trouble-free.

**Take care**
Keep plants moist. 144◗

# Tsuga canadensis 'Jeddeloh'

- **Partial shade**
- **Moist well-drained soil**
- **Slow-growing dwarf shrub**

This new cultivar makes a fine rockery plant, as it has a good lime-green colour and a semi-prostrate weeping habit, forming a flat bun-shape with a shallow hollow in the centre. As it is new, experts can only estimate its likely size; some say 50cm (20in) tall and 1m (39in) wide in ten years, but others say half this size, with an ultimate size of 1m (39in) high and 2m (6.5ft) across. The small flat leaves are ranged in rows along the sides and tops of the branches; these are densely packed, springing up and out from the centre, then curling down to give a neat shape of bright pale green.

The plant is propagated from cuttings; take these in autumn, set into a half peat and half sand mixture, and place in a cold frame over winter. In spring pot the rooted cuttings and plunge them into a nursery bed for three years. Plant out in shady positions in deep moist well-drained soil. These plants are trouble-free.

**Take care**
Weed and water young plants.

# Tsuga canadensis 'Pendula'

*(Weeping hemlock)*
- Sunshine or partial shade
- Moist well-drained soil
- Slow-growing medium shrub

This plant has a distinctive habit of growth, forming a mound of overlapping weeping branches, and it makes a fine specimen plant for the lawn, or set high on a rockery. It forms a shrub 1.5m (5ft) across in ten years; the height depends on whether the plant has been staked and trained, and with correct cultivation it should be around 1.5m (5ft) tall, but if left untrained it will remain a prostrate shrub 60cm (24in) high. A good plant should grow to 3m (10ft) tall and 9m (29.5ft) across. The foliage is mid-green and looks magnificent with the spring growth of pale lime-green tips.

It is propagated by cuttings taken in autumn, set in an equal mix of peat and sand, and put into a cold frame until spring. The rooted cuttings are put into pots and sunk into a nursery bed for three years. Plant out into the open or in partial shade in moist well-drained soil. Generally this shrub is trouble-free.

**Take care**
Protect from drying winds. 144♦

# Tsuga mertensiana 'Glauca'

- Sunshine or partial shade
- Well-drained moist soil
- Slow-growing large tree

This has a spire-like form, and although slow-growing, it will eventually make a large tree. In ten years it reaches 2m (6.5ft) tall with a spread of about 1m (39in); in 20 years it grows to 9m (29.5ft) tall and 4.5m (15ft) wide; and its ultimate height is 21m (70ft) in cultivation, although in the wild it can be twice this size. The foliage is a good blue colour with small flat leaves set radially around the stems. The branches are closely spaced from ground level to the top. Cones are borne on trees over 20 years old, and cluster at the top; they are 7.5cm (3in) long, and ripen to brown when ready to release the seeds.

To keep a good blue colour take cuttings in autumn, set in a half peat and half sand mixture and place in a cold frame for the winter. Pot up the rooted cuttings and plunge them into a nursery bed for three years. Plant out in sunlight or partial shade in a moist well-drained soil.

**Take care**
Keep young plants moist.

# Index of Common Names

# Credits

**Line artwork**
The drawings in this book have been prepared by Maureen Holt.
© Salamander Books Ltd.

**Photographs**
The photographs on pages 41 and 66 have been supplied by Michael Warren. The remaining photographs in the book have been taken by Eric Crichton and are
© Salamander Books Ltd.

**Editorial assistance**
Copy-editing and proof-reading: Maureen Cartwright.

**Acknowledgments**
The publishers would like to thank Blooms Nurseries, Bressingham, Norfolk for their help in location photography.

Below: *Cedrus atlantica*

PRINTED IN BELGIUM BY

INTERNATIONAL BOOK PRODUCTION

*Abies koreana 'Nana'*